PACIFIC GRAVEYARD

GRAVEYARD

*A narrative of the ships
lost where the Columbia River
meets the Pacific Ocean.*

By
JAMES A. GIBBS, JR.

BY THE PACIFIC

OREGON HISTORICAL SOCIETY

BINFORDS & MORT, Publishers
PORTLAND, OREGON

Printed in the United States of America
by
Binfords & Mort, Portland, Oregon

ACKNOWLEDGMENTS

————

My sincerest thanks are given to the Puget Sound Maritime Historical Society and to the Oregon Historical Society of which Lancaster Pollard is superintendent. I also wish to thank those good folks who live by the sea in Pacific County, namely, Charles Fitzpatrick, Charles Nelson and Mr. and Mrs. William Begg. Floyd M. Hecox, commanding officer of the Cape Disappointment Coast Guard Station, was most helpful. A debt of appreciation is also owed to the Corps of Engineers of the U. S. Army and to the U. S. Coast Guard. Last, but not least, I thank my mother who always kept the meals warm when I was late getting home.

To Cherie,

*who cheerfully stood by
the beachcomber who wrote
this epistle.*

CONTENTS

———

OCEAN SURF

CHAPTER ONE

IN THE BEGINNING

For a century and a half mariners have battled the vagaries of the temperamental Columbia River Bar. The waters over and about it have been the despair of seafarers. Those who work the bar are fully aware of the dangers, and though they curse its changeable personality, they have come to endure its nasty temper as a thing they must accept and outlast. Once proud ships are now twisted and gnarled tombstones in this graveyard, a section without parallel in ship disaster.

A constant contention between the river and the ocean has built obstructions between them which man has tried to break down. Like the peace maker, he has forced a truce between two unrelenting enemies;

1

but he has himself been made to pay a costly price in lives and property.

Through the ages the Columbia River has brought down to the bar sand and silt from an area larger than France. The tides of the Pacific meeting the river have built up deposits of sand covering a stretch of a hundred seacoast miles. To the south of the river entrance lies Clatsop Beach which reaches to Tillamook Head, a massive headland of rock. To the north spreads treacherous Peacock Spit, backed by the mighty bastion of Cape Disappointment, which is joined by North Head.

Still further north is a finger-shaped peninsula, one of the longest stretches of unbroken beach in the world; twenty-eight miles of sand indented only by Willapa bar at the northern extreme. Almost completely surrounded by water, the peninsula feels the constant roll of the ocean swell to the west, the hammering of the bar to the north and the shoal waters of the bay to the east.

Such is a sketch of the shore of lost ships. Here the ocean puts on her most striking show.

Every conceivable aid to navigation has been employed in this area, and continual vigils are maintained.

Since the turn of the century an estimated 60,000 ships have negotiated the bar, voyaging to and from all sectors of the globe. During this period man's continual fight to conquer the elements has limited the toll to about twenty-five major shipwrecks, approximately one-fourth as many as before.

Abounding in history, the Columbia River was only a rumor in the sixteenth century. Its existence was suggested by a Dutch chart of 1570 which listed a river in its approximate latitude. Many early explorers guessed that the finding of this river would mean the discovery of the fabled Northwest Passage.

The wealth of Spain in the sixteenth century supported a powerful fleet of galleons that sailed the seven seas in quest of new lands and treasure. Those ships voyaged to the New World and filled their holds with precious cargo for the mother country. Nor, so long as rumors of the River of the West existed was Spain content to conclude its expansion at Nueva Espana, and the exploration ships sailed up the North American Pacific coast.

One Spanish vessel is hazily recorded to have sailed as far north as the Columbia, since natives of the Clatsop plains have handed down a legend of a ship being cast ashore there about the year 1725.

The Spanish explorer, Martin d'Aguilar, makes reference to a probable river entrance seen on his voyage in 1603 while sailing off the Northwest Coast, but his records were vague. From this date there occurred a lapse of 170 years in the records of Spanish exploration along these shores. The search continued, but the existence of the river remained a mystery.

In 1775, Bruno Heceta, another of the family of Spanish explorers, sailed his ship, the *Santiago,* up to the mouth of a river, but being unable to find passage inward, concluded that it was of little importance and, after naming the headland at the north entrance St. Roc, sailed away.

The British sea rovers came next. It was Lieutenant John Meares who passed the fabled River of the West in 1788, in the ship *Felice,* after earlier charting Shoalwater Bay. Sailing near the coast on July 6, he named the indentation Deception Bay and changed Cape St. Roc on his charts to read Cape Disappointment, a title which expressed his chagrin at being unable to find an entrance.

Four years later Captain George Vancouver sailed near Cape Disappointment and, though he sighted breakers, attached little significance to a river opening and sailed northward to explore the waters of Puget Sound.

Strange indeed that, for all the explorers who searched for the river, it was discovered almost accidentally by a Yankee, Captain Robert Gray, a fur trader in quest of cargo for Boston merchants. He was first aware of the location while sailing southward from Vancouver Island in the early Spring of 1792. As he was passing within sight of the coast at 46° 14' North, he noticed breakers which he concluded must mark the shallow entrance to a river. His ship, the *Columbia* of Boston, sometimes called the *Columbia Rediviva,* made several attempts to cross the bar but was continually repelled by adverse currents. After nine days of waiting for the right slant of wind, Gray became discouraged and sailed for the Straits of Juan de Fuca. There he fell in company with Vancouver's three ships.

Gray and Vancouver exchanged information, but the Englishman refused to believe that an entrance to a river existed at the place where Gray had attempted a crossing.

Spurred by a greater determination to discover the river after his conversation with Vancouver, Gray again sailed southward.

On that historic voyage he discovered Bulfinch Harbor — now called Grays Harbor in his honor. Bearing still farther south, he approached Deception Bay, and launched his pinnace to sound the bar depths as the *Columbia* followed in its wake threading her way into the mouth of the great river. It was Friday, May 11, 1792, that Gray proudly sailed along the north banks of the river opening, naming the north entrance Cape Hancock and the southern tip Point Adams. To the long sought river he bestowed the name of his eighty-three-foot command. Gray had found the fabled River of the West, thereby opening it to the maritime nations of the world and bringing another nation into the contest for possession of the Northwest Coast.

Following Gray's ship by a few days came the British brig *Jenny* of Bristol, England, commanded by Captain James Baker, who received his share of glory by having the large bay at the north side of the river mouth named in his honor.

Upon learning of Gray's discovery, Vancouver dispatched Lieutenant William Broughton to sail for the river in the armed tender *Chatham* that was accompanying Vancouver's flagship *Discovery*. On October 20 of the same year the *Chatham* entered the river but stranded on the bar. Refloated with the flood tide she continued her voyage and anchored inside the mouth of the river, where preparations were made for surveying the channels. The vessel remained on the river until November 10, and then departed to rejoin Vancouver.

The first official survey of the river waited the arrival of Lieutenant Charles Wilkes of the United States Navy, in 1841. The mission suffered a setback when the USS *Peacock*, a unit of the squadron was carried on the north spit of the river entrance and totally wrecked. Peacock Spit, named for this early wreck, claimed numerous ships in the years that followed.

Among the findings of the Wilkes Expedition was the continual movement of the sands around the mouth of the river which, constantly changed the channel depths. This discovery revealed why it was so difficult to make accurate navigation charts of the bar.

Additional surveys of the Columbia were made in 1868 by the United States Coast Survey, and in 1876 by the United States Corps of Engineers. These surveys led to one conclusion: the need of a jetty as a permanent structure to keep the channel deep and stationary. After repeated petitions by Oregon citizens, a small sum for that work was finally appropriated in July, 1884, by the River and Harbor Bill.

Tons of rock were dumped to form a jetty across the south spit of the river in an attempt to harness several unreliable channels into one safe passage. The initial appropriation of $100,000, little more than got the work started. Several new appropriations were made and a period of ten years passed before the south jetty was finally completed.

The jetty eventually caused the treacherous middle sands to disappear, and where the controlling depths once varied between twenty and twenty-five feet, the river opening deepened considerably.

With the improving conditions another serious obstacle arose. While the south channel became deeper, the sands piled up on the north side of the river entrance.

Realizing the necessity of a north jetty, the government began construction on the project in 1914. The new jetty crossed Peacock Spit and extended for more than two miles to sea.

Today the depths of the bar are adequate and as many as 2,000 ships traverse the Columbia's portals annually. A competent staff of pilots is employed to guide ships over the bar.

Recent surveys show the project depths are forty feet deep from the river to Clatsop Spit buoy No. 14. The entrance is secured by the two converging rubble-mound jetties. The range of the tide between mean low water and mean high water is eight feet, while the controlling depth over the entrance bar is forty-five feet. These depths require the frequent work of an ocean-going hopper dredge which is operated by the Corps of Engineers, U. S. Army. Nearly $25,000,000 has been expended for the work and maintenance of the entrance to the Columbia and the lower river channels.

At the time of this writing the pilot schooner *Columbia*, stationed at the port of Astoria, has made approximately 40,000 crossings of the bar. She has been the official pilot boat since 1924. Her staunch wooden hull, tested in the ice packs of the frozen north in her early history, makes her an ideal ship for her duties.

With the end of World War II, an additional pilot vessel was needed and a former Navy motor minesweeper was rebuilt and commissioned as the *Peacock*.

The Columbia river has an average flow ranging between 90,000 and 1,000,000 cubic feet per second. It winds its way from the mountains to the sea over a distance of nearly 1400 miles and drains an area of about 259,000 square miles. In the calendar year of 1940, a total of 6,923,776 tons of traffic passed over the bar.

Though not accorded as great a place in history, Willapa Harbor has also played a prominent role in the maritime history of the Pacific Northwest. From these waters are picked the world famous Willapa oysters which thrive in the muddy sands that fill the lengthy bay, picturesque to view at high tide and equally as ugly on the ebb.

Flowing into the bay is the Willapa River, a lazy waterway on which the lumber towns of Raymond and South Bend are located. Across the bay on the lee side of the peninsula nestles the settlement of Oysterville, founded in 1854. That pioneer village, one of the oldest in the area, served as the county seat of Pacific County until the mushroom town of South Bend took over the honors in 1892. The rival community, pointing to promised railroad connections, swung the vote for the county seat but Oysterville residents protested the ballot, claiming that railroad workers voted illegally. Finally the South Benders invaded Oysterville and walked off with the legal records.

Land was first settled in the Willapa Bay area in

1845. Fifty-seven years earlier, Lieutenant John Meares, sailing in the ship *Felice*, discovered the entrance, but found it so guarded by heavy surf as not to warrant passage across the bar. Willapa Bay was originally named Shoalwater Bay, and was known as such until after the turn of the century.

Though no jetties have been constructed at the bar, dredging operations are carried on and the controlling depths range between twenty-two and twenty-five feet. There are two distinct channels used by vessels that negotiate Willapa bar. The entrance is marked by Leadbetter Point to the south and Cape Shoalwater to the north. Near the cape is the situation of the historic Willapa Bay Light Station, where a lookout tower was established in 1858. Some two million, two hundred thousand dollars has been expended on the maintenance and dredging of the bar, bay and channels which are navigable to three miles above Raymond.

In the year 1940, 292,269 tons of shipping crossed the bar with an additional 772,000 tons in rafting.

PEACOCK SPIT

CHAPTER TWO

VICTIMS OF THE TRANSPACIFIC DRIFT

Moving across the North Pacific in a sweeping semi-circle is a massive river within the ocean. Call it either the Japanese or the Pacific Current, it is one of the mainsprings of the entire Pacific current system, and is capable of carrying the most cumbersome objects on a one-way trip from Oriental shores.

It was this easterly drift that brought mysterious ships to America's shores long before the recorded appearance of the white man. It is further a possible explanation why traces of foreign blood were found among the natives of the Pacific Northwest by the early explorers.

Seventy-five Oriental junks are known to have been found adrift or ashore on the American side of the

9

Pacific up to the year 1875. As late as 1927 a disabled Japanese fishing boat, containing a crew of dead men, was picked up off Cape Flattery, Washington.

Among the early Pacific sea merchants were the Spanish who established trading between Mexico and the Philippines in the seventeenth century. It is believed by historians that their ships reached our shores on several occasions after falling victim to the adverse winds and the prevailing northerly currents that mark the Pacific's seacoast.

As told by the descendents of the Clatsop tribe, of the Oregon Country, a weather-beaten and waterlogged vessel was sighted wallowing in the surf south of the entrance to the Columbia years before the recorded arrival of white explorers. According to the legend, it was strawberry time and a south wind howled across the mouth of the river. The natives eyed the strange craft, but believing it to be an evil omen, hastily returned to their village.

When dawn sent its light across the sky, a flickering fire crackled on the beach. Around the fire huddled the figures of two castaways. From their pale faces grew beards and from their hands extended sticks which they were using to pop corn over the fire. Down among the breakers wedged in the sand the remains of their ship rested as the tide ebbed and flowed through her timbers.

From the top of a crested dune a Clatsop woman appeared while making her morning rounds in search of driftwood. Her black eyes followed along the beach and came to rest upon the castaways. She turned and ran back to the ancient village of Ne-ahkstow as fast as her legs would carry her.

"Strangers on the beach which look like bears and yet are men," she yelled as she ran.

Pandemonium broke loose in the village and the tribesmen armed themselves and began rushing toward the beach. The native woman pointed out the spot where she had seen the strange men and the tribe approached with caution.

Never before had they seen long beards, white skin or the popping corn by which the strangers were fed.

As the Clatsop Chieftain stepped forward to inspect the intruders he kept muttering, "Tlo-hon-nipts," which is to say, "those who drift ashore from the sea." Putting forth his stubby hands he closely examined the heads of the castaways to see if they resembled his own head. When satisfied that they were men and not animals, he held a short consultation with his tribe and then announced that he would claim the strangers as slaves.

Too exhausted to resist, the shipwrecked sailors resigned themselves to their fate.

As the tide receded, the wreck was left high on the beach and the natives swarmed over her sides removing the loose gear. They found that the ship's interior contained boxes of supplies including trinkets and strings of beads which greatly pleased the plunderers.

The two captives were taken back to the village and fed until they regained their strength. Later they were put to work at hard labor.

It was discovered that one of the captives had a talent for making knives and other implements of iron. This gained him considerable favor with the tribe and the name Konapee, "the iron worker," was conferred upon him.

The Clatsops returned again and again to the scene of the wreck to remove the copper sheathing and iron fastenings which they promptly brought to Konapee. Finally the ship's remains were burned to recover the last remains of metal.

The tribal chief informed Konapee that in turn for making knives and tools for the natives he and his companion would be given their freedom. Konapee was

permitted to select a site for his home and chose a location near what was later known as Point Adams.

Clatsop legend fails to reveal the plight of Konapee's
companion, but it appears that the iron worker lived
alone, for long after his death the natives referred to
the site of his home as the place of Konapee. Even after
the white settlers came to the Columbia, the name was
still held in high favor by the natives.

One legend claims that Konapee's companion was
sold to the Willapa tribe, situated north of the Columbia River.

Cherished among the Clatsops for years was some
Chinese money that had been in the possession of
Konapee when he was shipwrecked. It was referred to
as Konapee's money, and led early historians to believe
that the two survivors were Orientals. Though numerous junks drifted across the Pacific it is more likely
that the vessel in question was of Spanish origin.

Chinese currency was often found among the Span-
iards, who traded with the Philippines and China in
those early years. Further upholding the suggestion
of a Spanish ship, was the presence of beards on the
faces of the castaways, which would not have been
found on Orientals. The Indian corn doubtless came
from Mexico.

The presence of white men once or twice removed
were found among the coast natives when Lewis and
Clark came west in 1805.

Stories concerning the offsprings of Konapee have
long been related. As far back as 1814, an old Indian
was found at the Cascades, in Oregon, who claimed to
be the son of a Spaniard who had survived a shipwreck
near the mouth of the Columbia River. He gave his
nas as Soto and in all probability he was Konapee's
son, as his story coincided with the Clatsop legend of
the shipwreck. The age of Soto was reputed to be about
eighty years, which would have meant that Konapee

was cast ashore on Clatsop Beach, about 1725. This was perhaps the first landing of white men among the natives at the mouth of the Columbia.

Indian legend mentions two other landings of white men in the seventeenth or eighteenth centuries along the Oregon coast, both of which occurred several miles south of the Columbia in the Nehalem country. One incident is referred to as the "Beeswax ship" and the other as the "Treasure ship."

In the year 1820, a Japanese junk was cast upon the sands near Point Adams, after drifting across the Pacific. The craft was discovered by two Clatsops who approached the wreck and crawled over her slimy timbers. The faint scent of incense permeated the cabin, but the crew and supplies were missing.

There is always the essence of romance and mystery connected with the odyssey of an abandoned ship, but the junk that came ashore in 1820 was only one of the many wrecked on the American shores during Japan's exclusion from the outside world.

The currents of the Pacific took their toll in the early periods of exploration.

THE BEAVER

CHAPTER THREE

INDIAN TROUBLES

With the beginning of the nineteenth century a new era was opened through the portals of the Columbia River. Streams rich in beaver attracted traders to gather furs highly valued in world markets, and later tall timber and productive valleys brought settlers. Between the natives and the white men oc-

14

casionally misunderstandings arose which often had bloody aftermaths.

When the mystery junk of 1820 was cast ashore at Point Adams, twenty-eight years had passed since Gray's discovery of the Columbia. Traders were sailing their ships into its waters. Within five years the Hudson's Bay Company would establish Fort Vancouver one hundred miles up stream.

The Ship *Tonquin*

Astoria was established through the plans of John Jacob Astor, business tycoon and fur trader of New York. He organized one party to go overland and another by sea to locate a suitable spot for a trading post at the mouth of the Columbia.

In command of Captain Jonathan Thorn, the ten-gun ship *Tonquin* departed New York on September 8, 1810, with thirty-three colonizers and sufficient supplies for the new Astor colony. The vessel's master was a Naval officer, relieved from his commission to perform this special duty. He governed his command with an iron hand. The passengers were French Canadian fur-traders not accustomed to such discipline. Trouble started shortly after the voyage began. Before the *Tonquin* reached the Sandwich Islands, mutiny and murder had been narrowly averted.

After a brief stay in the Islands to replenish stores, the *Tonquin* departed for the Columbia River. Twenty-three days later, on March 22, 1811, the vessel arrived at the river entrance. Thorn, anxious to land his mutinous party, took few precautions as he neared the bar. To further complicate matters the entrance was rough with breakers caused by a strong southwest wind. Unfamiliar with the bar conditions, Thorn ordered his first officer, William Fox, and four of the ship's company, to man the whaleboat and take soundings.

Fox, aware that the craft was in serious need of re-
pair, requested that he be given one of the other boats.

"If you are afraid of the sea, Mr. Fox, you should
have never left Boston," replied the Captain.

With that the boat went over the side into the heaving swells. Fox at the tiller, the craft moved over the
bar but disappeared and was never seen again.

Nightfall came on and the ship rolled violently in
the sea. The following day the wind subsided and the
Tonquin found anchorage in fourteen fathoms near
the north entrance of the river, but had yet to cross
the bar.

The presence of the *Tonquin* aroused the attention
of the natives along the shores and they prepared their
canoes to come out and barter if the ship entered the
river.

Still lying in a dangerous position, it was decided
that Alexander McKay and David Stuart of the Astor
party should man the pinnace and sound the bar channel. The boat was lowered, but within a few minutes
swamped in the surf and the two men narrowly escaped with their lives.

The pinnace was bailed out and repaired and another attempt was made to sound the bar which also
ended in failure. The *Tonquin* was slowly being carried toward the shore and Captain Thorn found his
position growing more perilous by the hour.

Among the cargo carried on the vessel was the frame
of a small schooner which was to have been assembled
at the new establishment. All hands set to work and
shortly had the craft fitted together. John Aiken was
put in charge and was assisted by the ship's sailmaker
and the ship's armourer. When the work was completed the vessel was manned for one final attempt to
guide the *Tonquin* into safe waters.

The schooner proved to be more successful than the
smaller boats and eventually located the safe channel.

Carefully marking the area, the craft started back to join the *Tonquin,* but the currents swept her broadside into a curling breaker, tossing her on her beam ends and spilling the crew into the chilling waters.

Thorn would not risk sending aid to the struggling men, as he needed every hand to save the ship from being carried on the spit. Suddenly the *Tonquin* struck, and water surged over her decks and loose gear floated free of its fittings. Shrouds and halyards snapped as the vessel kept poking her prow on the shoal. Foundering seemed imminent and fear filled the vessel's company.

Almost miraculously the *Tonquin* drifted free with the tide and was carried over the bar after having struck it repeatedly without sustaining serious damage to her hull.

At daybreak the natives came alongside in their canoes. Barter, however, failed to interest the crew, for they mourned the loss of their shipmates and immediately set out to comb the shore in the hope of finding them alive. Stephen Weekes, the armourer, and one of the Kanaka sailors who had joined the ship in the islands, were found near Cape Disappointment, suffering from exposure; but the search failed to locate the others. The schooner was washed ashore and later rebuilt at the new settlement and named *Dolly*.

While the *Tonquin* lay at anchor off the north bank of the river the Astor party set out in search of a suitable location for a post. Finally a sight was selected at Point George—so named by Lieutenant Broughton several years earlier. That location on the south bank offered protection from the winds and a sheltered moorage.

For the next several days all hands were busied unloading the cargo of the *Tonquin* while the natives gathered near, filled with curiosity. By June 5 the stevedoring duties were completed and the vessel weighed anchor. Bidding farewell to the colonizers the ship's company departed for Vancouver Island in quest of a cargo of furs. Enroute to sea, a native came alongside in a small dugout and asked to be taken on the voyage to act as interpreter. He gave his name as Lamazee, and claimed to be well acquanited with the tribes to the north. Considering him a valuable addition to the crew, Captain Thorn granted him passage and the ship continued her voyage.

More than a year later this same native, face drawn and naked body bruised, entered the gates of Astoria. He claimed to be the sole survivor of the *Tonquin's* party.

In the story he told, the *Tonquin* had entered Clayoquot Harbor on Vancouver Island and anchored off the village of Neweetee. The natives were filled with anxiety as their canoes came out to meet the ship. When bartering began, a wrinkled old chief named Nookamis was allowed to come aboard to display his pelts. Nookamis had become shrewd in his methods of bargaining after dealings with earlier white traders and refused all offers made by Thorn. The ship's master became enraged with the persistant chief and threw him overboard.

Pretending to continue bartering the following day, the natives, enraged by the incident of the preceeding day, boarded the *Tonquin* with their skins. At a given signal they commenced an attack on the crew which left the ship's decks running with blood. Only four escaped by managing to reach the after cabin and holding the savages off with rifle fire. Captain Thorn and the others were murdered.

Being a native, Lamazee was unharmed, but was forced to flee with the attackers to escape the bullets fired by the surviving crew members.

Lacking sufficient man power to operate the ship, three members of the crew attempted an escape by lifeboat during the night. Repelled by a strong wind at the harbor entrance they sought refuge in a cave on the shore, but were discovered by the natives and taken back to the village where they were tortured to death.

Mr. Lewis, the ship's clerk, kept a lonely vigil aboard the *Tonquin*. Wounded in the skirmish, he had refused to join his shipmates in their escape. Intent on revenge he paced the debris laden deck hour after hour making friendly signs to the natives to come on board.

Growing increasingly confident the savages swarmed up over the sides of the vessel from scores of canoes and set about to strip the ship of its wares. With the decks teeming with excited red men. Lewis, unnoticed, slipped down to the ship's powder magazine and ignited it.

For an instant there was a twisting flame and a puff of smoke followed by a tremendous explosion. Bodies went spinning through the air and fell into the sea. The *Tonquin* was blasted into pieces along with the nearby war canoes. Bodies washed up on the beaches for days after.

At the conclusion of his story Lamazee estimated that more than five-score natives were killed and many others were maimed for life as a result of the explosion.

Bark *William and Ann*

Firmly established in 1825, Fort Vancouver, the Hudson's Bay Company post, became a mecca for fur traders in the nineteenth century. Numerous ships from the United Kingdom arrived on the river to bring supplies and return home with furs. American ships were sent to the river by eastern merchants who carried on a thriving trade to the Orient.

There was cause for celebration each time a vessel arrived from far ports; but when disaster was reported gloom fell over the settlers, for it meant the loss of essential supplies.

In early March of 1829 the British bark *William and Ann*, owned by the Hudson's Bay Company, arrived off the mouth of the Columbia, after a long voyage from London. Falling in company with the American schooner *Convoy*, of Boston, Captain Thompson, master, the two vessels maneuvered for the crossing of the bar. Coming in on a port tack the *Convoy* entered first as her crew sounded the depths at frequent intervals. When the schooner had cleared the bar, the velocity of the wind had increased two-fold, and refuge was taken in Bakers Bay.

The *William and Ann* was nowhere in sight. After several hours of scanning the horizon, the schooner's lookout yelled from aloft, "The Britisher's in trouble, Sir."

Without hesitation, Captain Thompson called for volunteers, and soon the ship's boat put out to sea to aid the stricken vessel. Pulling to within a quarter of a mile of the *William and Ann*, the would-be rescuers became exhausted in their battle against the sea and were forced to abandon the effort and return to the *Convoy*.

All night the storm raged. Trapped in the sands off Clatsop Spit, the *William and Ann* was pounded by overflowing walls of water and her total complement of forty-six persons was carried into the sea.

When the *Convoy* anchored off Fort George—as Astoria was then called—word was received that the Clatsops were salvaging large quantities of goods washed on the beach in the aftermath of the wreck. When that news was sent to Fort Vancouver a party was immediately organized for a visit to the Clatsop village to recover the goods. The natives made no attempt to hide their gifts from the sea, for when the Hudson's Bay Company party entered the village they found a grand array of supplies as well as wooden crates stamp-marked, "London, England." A demand was made of the chief for the return of the goods, but it was denied. Instead, the high ranking native handed the white leader a tattered old broom instructing him to return it to Dr. John McLoughlin, then in charge of Fort Vancouver.

"You tell white leader he receive no more," muttered the chief.

Too small to enforce their demands the party departed. They presented the broom to McLoughlin on their return, after which plans were made to send an armed party to the village to regain the merchandise by force if necessary.

Meanwhile McLoughlin was informed that an abandoned lifeboat from the *William and Ann* was in the possession of the Clatsops, and gossip that the natives had murdered the survivors was circulated at the settlement. The stories gained impetus and the post was burning for revenge.

In the fall of the year a small river schooner was armed with cannon and filled with colonizers, ready to do battle with the Clatsops. The plan called for one group to go by land while the other attacked the village from the water. When the schooner approached the area it sent a volley from the cannon into the center of the village. The Clatsops were taken by complete surprise. They fled to the forests to protect themselves, but in the cross-fire from the land army one of the natives was killed and two others injured.

The battle was over and the Fort Vancouver party walked into the village and recovered the loot.

Some of the tribe were taken as hostages and questioned over the murder of the survivors of the *William and Ann*, but each emphatically insisted that the lifeboat was found abandoned.

The attack on the village was severely criticized by

the Americans, but the conquerors stressed the fact
that the incident taught the natives respect for the
Hudson's Bay Company power and property.

SAND ISLAND

CHAPTER FOUR

SAND

Noah Webster describes sand as the more or less fine debris of rocks, consisting of small loose grains often of quartz as is found on a beach.

The hard-shelled skipper of an old square rigger, on finding his ship aground on a shoal, might have had a slightly different definition—which cannot be repeated in these lines.

Sand, as harmless as it appears, has been a prime factor in the destruction of most of the ships lost in the Pacific Graveyard. It is capable of sucking its prey down and devouring the remains like a hungry animal.

An enormous sand deposit was found at the mouth of the Columbia by the early navigators. This deposit

23

was constantly shifted by the conflict of river flow and ocean storm. Channels varying in depth from nineteen to thirty feet were formed and again effaced. Tens of millions of cubic yards were moved into a given area, or out again within a few seasons.

Along the coastline southward, a steadily narrowing sand spit or beach extends from the Columbia River to Tillamook Head, beyond which it all but disappears. The beaches to the north, however, increase in importance. Submerged bars and spits project prominently at Willapa Bay and Grays Harbor entrances, having been formed without the assistance of silt or sediment carrying rivers emptying into these entrances. Therefore the Columbia River becomes the artery of the sand conditions along the shores of Oregon and Washington.

The fine sand found around the Columbia's portal, readily shifted from point to point by the combined action of wind, tide and currents, is carried northward by a prevailing northerly drift.

British Bark *Isabella*

Another of the fleet of ships operating between London and the Pacific Northwest was the British bark *Isabella,* commanded by Captain Thomas Ryan. Arriving in May of 1830, the vessel stood in to the Columbia River bar bearing cargo for Fort Vancouver.

All went well till the wind slackened and the vessel lost headway. There was a heavy swell on the bar and the currents were strong. The sails fell limp and the falling glass in the master's cabin warned of an approaching storm. The current carried the ship from the channel and put her on the shoal off treacherous Sand Island. Both anchors were dropped to hold her steady. Kedging was attempted but this proved futile as the vessel held to her grip on the sands,

A sharp wind blew from the southwest and the

breakers pounded the stern of the *Isabella,* hollowing out the sand from around her hull. When the mate reported that the ship was taking water rapidly, fear spread among the crew lest the same misfortune befall them that did the complement of the *William and Ann.* Captain Ryan was forced to deal harshly with them to dispel their anxiety to abandon ship.

Though indications pointed towards disaster, the ship's master was still hopeful of saving his vessel until the carpenter reported that she was badly holed and breaking up. Having no other alternative, Ryan ordered the ship abandoned. The crew lowered the boats and gave a lusty pull for the beach.

Intent on returning to the wreck after the wind had abated, Captain Ryan awaited daybreak, but all that remained of the *Isabella* was a tangled mass of wreckage. He was criticized for abanding his command before the change of the tide as the vessel might possibly have been floated free with the efforts of all hands.

Sloop of War *Peacock*

Another decade slipped by before serious disaster again occurred on the Columbia bar. On July 18, 1841, the U.S. Naval brig *Peacock* ended the period of safe bar transit. The eighteen-gun sloop of war was a unit of Lieutenant Charles Wilkes' Expedition employed in sounding and charting Pacific Ocean waters.

When the *Peacock,* Captain William L. Hudson, master, arrived off the mouth of the Columbia from the Sandwich Islands, the sky was clear and flaked with puffs of clouds: the bar was favorable for crossing, but Captain Hudson carried only inaccurate bar charts given him by Captain Josiah Spaulding of the ship *Lausanne* while in the Islands.

The chart was followed closely but the main channel was erroneously marked and the vessel struck the sands with a terrific impact. The tide was ebbing and the freshening breeze sent volumes of water smashing against the ship. Her beamy hull pounded on the sand like a sledge hammer. A comber leaped over the vessel and crushed the ship's cutter. The crew were ordered to jettison all excess cargo in an attempt to free the ship. Over went the cannons, the shot, and the stores. The port anchor was dropped, and by herculean efforts the vessel's head was turned toward the open sea.

Any hope that may have come at that moment faded as the anchor chain snapped, forcing the *Peacock* to turn broadside, yawing in the surf. By midnight the crew were sloshing around in three feet of water on the gun deck. They were cold and exhausted and all chances of escaping in the ship's launch were useless in the face of the rising sea. The pumps which were manned continuously finally became clogged with debris and had to be abandoned.

By 6 a.m. the sea had calmed considerably and a native war canoe carrying a pilot from Fort George pushed its way out to the side of the vessel. The pilot's arrival was to no avail, for during the night the brig's hull had broken under the strain of working on the shoal and all hands had elected to abandon ship.

While carrying the crew members ashore on the second trip, the *Peacock's* launch capsized in a breaker and ten seamen were thrown into the swell and narrowly escaped with their lives.

Captain Hudson was the last to leave the ship and with him went the *Peacock's* articles and navigation instruments.

The following day the *Peacock* broke up and her wreckage was scattered along the shore. Her grave was marked only by her bowsprit which protruded from the sands.

When Lieutenant Wilkes arrived at Fort George aboard the USS *Porpoise*, he chartered the American schooner *Thomas H. Perkins,* at anchor off the settlement, and placed the *Peacock's* crew aboard to continue survey work on the river.

Before departing the Columbia, Wilkes found that there was no space to carry the *Peacock's* launch and decided to leave it at Fort George where it could be maintained as a rescue boat for the relief of vessels in distress.

French Bark *Morning Star*

She flew the French flag and in gold gilt across her counter read the name *Morning Star*. She hailed from Le Havre and had arrived off the mouth of the Columbia in July, 1849, after a seven months passage.

A week passed and the vessel still waited outside the river for the arrival of a pilot, but none came. Her master, Captain Francis Menes, grew impatient. He was a big man whose ruddy face was framed from ear to ear with a flaming red beard. He spoke an American brig outbound from the river on the eighth day and was informed that no pilot was available.

Meanwhile, a coastwise schooner arrived off the river and again the *Morning Star* exchanged information. Menes learned that a few months earlier one of the bar pilots had piled the British bark *Vancouver* on the middle sands and to avoid embarrassing questions had departed for San Francisco.

That was the last straw, and the French skipper on the first favorable wind got his command under way. Not entirely unfamiliar with the bar, Captain Menes had successfully crossed it on a voyage two years earlier. He had kept notes on his first crossing, but was unaware of the changing conditions of the bar entrances. On July 11, the *Morning Star* started the inbound trek, heavily laden and drawing sixteen feet. Off Sand Island, the vessel struck the bottom. The enraged skipper, who had been following his charts with precision, stormed to the taffrail, gazed overboard and tossed his charts into the surf.

For ten hours the vessel was hung up on the spit. Working on the sands the timbers were loosened and water began pouring through her seams. The boats were lowered but as fast as they hit the water they were destroyed in the tempest. When the last remaining lifeboat went over the side a seaman volunteered to hold it steady until his shipmates could man the craft. He was unaware of a giant wave that rolled toward the boat as it dangled in the davits, and the howl of the wind blotted out the warnings of the crew. The comber struck with such force that it literally swallowed up the boat and its occupant.

With the last boat gone all hope for rescue faded. The wreck was at the mercy of the buffeting seas. Stern first on the shoal, the rudder cracked under the strain and drifted free of the vessel. A moment later a section of the keel parted and to the amazement of the crew, the bark released its grip on the spit and drifted into the channel as if guided by an unseen hand. She came drifting into Bakers Bay several hours later with her exhausted crew draped over the rigging, seemingly more dead than alive.

John Lattie, a bar pilot from the Astor settlement, sighted the derelict and made haste to the vessel's side with several natives in a canoe. Following him came the crews of three sailing vessels that were at anchor in the river, the ship *Walpole*, the brig *Undine* and the bark *John W. Carter*. The salvagers scrambled aboard the *Morning Star* and began clearing the tangled rigging in an effort to get at the pumps and save the ship from sinking. The exhausted Frenchmen were taken ashore while the salvage gang worked ceaselessly for twenty-four hours before the vessel's holds were finally emptied of water. When the task was completed, a box rudder was installed and the ship taken up river to Portland, where the damaged cargo was disposed of at high prices. The hull was later sold to the firm of Couch and Flanders, of Portland, who later resold it to California interests.

That she ever went to sea again is doubtful.

American Bark *Mindora*

On January 12, 1853, double tragedy occurred on the Columbia bar with the loss of two American vessels, the barks *Mindora* and *I. Merrithew*.

The more important of the two wrecks from a historical standpoint is the loss of the *Mindora,* a 400 ton coastwise vessel, which was enroute to Portland from San Francisco when disaster occurred. While some of the most severe weather of the year blew itself out, the *Mindora* was compelled to wait outside the bar for twenty-eight days. One gale after another lashed the shores and the bar was a foaming mass of swells. Food and supplies ran short on the vessel and her master, Captain George Staples, was forced to ration the water, hardtack and beans. The crew became quarrelsome, and all that kept them in line was the presence of a few other vessels that had arrived off the bar and were undergoing similar trials.

On January 12, a temporary calm prevailed and the *Mindora* trimmed sail for the crossing. Making good headway with a running sea the vessel pitched gently at four knots when suddenly the wind died completely, forcing the square rigger to anchor off Sand Island. Her position was exposed to the currents, which started her anchors dragging in spite of efforts by the crew to hold her position. The currents carried the vessel toward the middle sands and beached her on a shoal. The vessel shuddered under the strain and no sooner had she struck than the breakers swept her decks, smashing the housing aft and flooding the foc'sle forward.

The crewmen held their stations until Captain Staples gave the order to abandon, and then manned a boat and launched out into the tempest. Icy water poured into the craft as fast as eager hands could bail it out. With a sailor's will they rowed, tossing about as the darkness closed in around them. All the way to Astoria they went, backs and arms at the breaking point and the boat with only a few inches of freeboard.

When help arrived with food and warm clothing the crew members were so exhausted that for several hours they slept stretched out around the pot belly stove in the town hall.

In the morning Captain Staples summoned the pilot schooner and shoved off from Astoria to find the wreck. When they arrived at the scene all that greeted their eyes was an empty stretch of sand. The *Mindora* was nowhere to be found. First conclusions were that she had foundered and was buried in the sands, but the true story was not learned until several days later.

The *Mindora* wasn't ready to terminate her career of roaming the seas and after being abandoned decided to set her own course. During the night the vessel pounded on the sands until her anchor cables parted. The sands were hollowed from her hull by the surging tides and the currents swept her out to sea. Like a ghost ship she drifted in the murk. Her masts were severed from their fittings and wreckage covered her decks, but the vessel drifted on, nobody ever knowing how far.

The *Mindora* might have joined the legendary world of phantom ships, but that several days later her battered hulk plowed its way through the breakers and came to rest on the beach several miles north of Shoalwater Bay.

An interesting conclusion to this story is the tale of the bark *I. Merrithew*, lost at the bar on the same day as the *Mindora*. Earlier the two vessels had loaded side by side in San Francisco Bay, and both departed for the river within a few days of each other. They crossed the bar on the same day and both came to grief. No loss of life occurred in either wreck. As did the *Mindora*, the *I. Merrithew*, which grounded on Clatsop Spit, drifted to sea after being abandoned. The latter vessel's trip was curtailed when she was swept against the rock walls near North Head.

American Bark *Desdemona*

Many of the spits and sand bars at the mouth of the Columbia have been named for the ships that have stranded on them. One such unlucky ship was the bark *Desdemona*. Though many of these shoals have been effaced, Desdemona Sands are still in existence today. They were charted after the *Desdemona* left her bones there on New Year's Day in 1857.

Captain Francis Williams made a wager before his vessel departed San Francisco. It was the price of a new Sunday suit to be given him by the vessel's owner, Thomas Smith, if he could get his cargo to the river by New Year's Day. Williams had faith in the *Desdemona*, and her owner stood to gain a handsome price from the consignee if the cargo arrived on time.

The *Desdemona* was one of the most familiar ships in the coasting trade and one of the most dependable. She was built at Jonesboro, Maine, in 1847, and had been operating out of the Columbia River since 1851.

Captain Williams didn't spare an inch of canvas on the northbound trip and arrived off the mouth of the river in good time. It was New Year's eve towards midnight, but the *Desdemona's* master preferred not to cross the bar until dawn. Deep in the water with a heavy load of general merchandise, every precaution would have to be taken to safeguard the vessel in bar transit. When daybreak came the *Desdemona* signalled for a pilot. When the pilot boat failed to come, Williams decided to save the vessel's owner the fee and take her into the river himself. His knowledge of the bar was adequate but his vessel set deep in the water and the swell on the bar caused her to labor heavily. Suddenly the ship struck at a spot where the charts had indicated deep water.

Concerned over the valuable cargo, Williams ordered a boat lowered and he and some of the ship's crew went to Astoria to seek aid. While they were away the U. S. Revenue Cutter *Joe Lane* hove too and got a line aboard the stricken craft. For hours the cutter strained to free the *Desdemona*, but abandoned the effort after the third hawser had parted.

When Williams returned to his ship he brought several men from the Parker Sawmill to help refloat her, but much to his dismay discovered that his vessel had bilged and was sinking deeper in the sands. All hands set to work removing the cargo in lighters. They worked night and day until January 3, when the pilot boat arrived and warned them of an approaching storm. The crew went ashore until the winds had died, and then returned two days later to finish the job with the aid of a wooden scow. Anxious to complete the task the scow was overloaded and when a snorting tug from the mill arrived it had difficulty controlling it against the currents. The scow began to roll at dangerous angles and then she swamped and capsized throwing her cargo and several of the *Desdemona's* crew into the water. One of the seamen was trapped beneath the scow and drowned, but the others struggled in the water until the tug managed to pick them up.

At a public auction in Astoria on January 6, the wreck of the *Desdemona* brought only $215. She was sold to Moses Rogers who stripped the hull of everything removable.

For many years the ribs of the *Desdemona* were pointed out to passengers crossing the bar. Finally one hard winter the wreck sank deep in the sands and has never been seen since.

Before a hearing involving the loss of his ship, Captain Williams claimed that the wreck was caused by the absence of the lower bar buoy which was reported missing from position when the *Desdemona* was inbound.

Whether or not he ever got his new suit has always remained a mystery.

American Bark *Industry*

Inscribed on Shark Rock, on Niagara Street in Astoria, is an epitaph telling of the loss of the American bark *Industry*, lost, as was the brig *S. D. Lewis*, on March 16, 1865, another double tragedy day on the Columbia bar.

The *Industry* was a coastwise trader built at Stockton, Maine, by Captain Paul Corno, who earlier had amassed a fortune with his initial vessel, the brig *Susan Abigale*. The new Corno addition had paid for herself within a few months of her arrival on the Pacific Coast. Her record was unmarred until her fatal voyage from San Francisco to Portland in command of Captain I. Lewis.

Departing the Golden Gate February 23, the *Industry* shoved off on a hectic voyage up the coast. Several days later she arrived off the river badly battered by the succession of gales she had encountered. Some of her crew had been injured by the heavy seas and her fresh water tanks had been smashed.

The bar was rough and the pilot boat was nowhere in sight, but the barkentine *Falkenberg* was sighted nearby and hailed by Captain Lewis. He made an urgent plea for fresh water and after the seas had calmed a boat was lowered and eventually returned with casks full of the precious liquid.

No pilot came, and Lewis determined to assume the responsibility for his vessel, ordered the sail trimmed as she moved in for the crossing.

"Sail Ho!" yelled a seaman from aloft.

"Where away?" came the answer from the ship's master.

"Two points off the starboard bow."

It was the pilot boat and as it approached the *Industry*, a signal flag was raised. Presuming that he was to alter his course Lewis waited for the pilot schooner to come alongside but instead it turned about and started back across the bar. It was evident that the *Industry* was expected to follow in her wake.

When well underway the wind failed and the bark was obliged to drop her anchors and stay clear of the sands. Within fifteen minutes the breeze returned and the hooks were weighed. For five minutes more the vessel groped her way along the bar when the wind died once again. Again the anchors went over the side but the vessel had already lost steerageway and was drifting into shallow water. A moment later she struck stern first near the middle sands, severing her rudder.

The vessel finally freed herself and began drifting over the spit. Desperate attempts were made to clear the sands, but less than 100 yards further she drove ashore again, this time dislodging her false keel.

Fearing for the lives of his passengers, Captain Lewis ordered a boat lowered and placed first officer Coppin in charge. Before the passengers could man it, a giant swell flipped the craft skyward tearing out the bottom and sweeping Coppin to a watery grave. No further attempts were made to lower another boat as the sea was running and the wind increasing.

As night approached on the wings of a gale, all hands

took to the rigging like spiders in a web. The rising seas stove in the boats, up-rooted the capstan and carried the steering wheel and the binnacle into the deep. Tons of water cascaded over the vessel as it settled. After seemingly eternal night, daylight shed its light on a battered and broken ship inhabited by gaunt figures of human life.

Though they were chilled to the bone, Captain Lewis ordered the crew and passengers to set to work building rafts as the one remaining means of saving their lives. With the decks awash they worked ceaselessly, constructing one raft from fallen yardarms and the other from wooden pumps.

The first conveyance was set adrift with five persons aboard and was carried over the bar where a lifeboat manned by soldiers from Fort Stevens rescued them. The second raft met with ill fortune when four men were swept overboard and drowned while a fifth died of exposure. A pretty twelve-year-old girl was also carried overboard and perished after frantic efforts to save her had failed. Only two of the passengers out of the eight that took passage on the *Industry* reached shore alive.

Some of the ship's crew remained with the wreck so that the others could have a place on the rafts. They too met death when the vessel broke up shortly after the second raft set out to cross the bar.

Probably the incident is best described on Shark Rock, in these simple words: "The bark *Industry* was lost March 16, 1865; lives lost 17, saved 7."

American Steamer *Great Republic*

One of the wrecks still talked about by old-time captains was that of the side-wheel passenger steamer *Great Republic*. She entered the coastwise run in 1878, as the largest passenger steamer on the Pacific Coast. She was owned by P. B. Cornwall and successfully operated until she stranded on Sand Island, April 19, 1879, with a loss of eleven lives.

The *Great Republic* was constructed at Greenport, Long Island, New York, in 1866, for the historic Pacific Mail Steamship Company. Built of white oak and chestnut, the vessel was strengthened with copper and iron fastenings. She measured 378 feet in length and registered 4750 gross tons.

For several years the vessel was in the China trade, but she was a costly ship to operate, and as her owners could not meet expenses they decided to lay her up at San Francisco.

Cornwall, an adventurer as well as a promoter, eyed the *Great Republic* and decided to purchase her for coast passenger service. He acquired her for a fraction of her original cost. His plan was to worry the other coastwise steamship companies into paying him to keep his ship off the run. The scheme failed to materialize, however, and his only alternative was to give the vessel

STEAMER *GREAT REPUBLIC*

a face-lifting and place her in the passenger and freight service between San Francisco and Portland.

Cornwall found to his surprise that business was booming. On the *Great Republic's* initial voyage she carried 225 passengers and more than 400 tons of freight.

On her arrival at Portland, June 19, 1878, the big vessel was given a warm welcome. Portlanders turned out in large numbers to salute the big ship and to fete her master, Captain James Carroll.

She carried 236 passengers on the return trip to San Francisco, and for the next six passages more than 600 passengers and 500 tons of freight in spite of a rate war promoted by her competitors.

The *Great Republic* was also a fast carrier. Her vertical beam engine, fed by four massive boilers, made more than one old river skipper scratch his head in amazement when he heard she had run from Portland to Astoria in five hours and fifteen minutes.

It was a happy crowd of some 896 passengers that departed San Francisco in the spring of 1879. The *Great Republic,* including her crew, carried more than 1,000 persons.

At midnight on April 18, the steamer arrived off the mouth of the Columbia. The pilot boat was awaiting her arrival and pulled alongside to put pilot Thomas Doig aboard. Doig decided to await daylight before taking the steamer across but later changed his plans. At 12:30 a.m. the vessel's course was set.

Passengers were sleeping soundly in their berths, oblivious to the ship's slow pitch in the long swells. It was high tide and the sea was calm. The pilot guided the steamer as far as the Sand Island buoy and then suddenly the ship came to a stop with a jolt.

Only some of the more curious passengers bothered to come up on deck to see what had happened. The *Great Republic* was aground on Sand Island, but word was spread among the tourists that the vessel would be refloated with the following tide. Unfortunately the ship hit the shoal at the extreme tide and the ebb left her in a position that severely tested her hull. She was such a cumbersome vessel that the strain forward and aft played amidships and disconnected the steam pipes.

The sea was rising and the bilge pumps clogged with silt were failing to function properly, allowing the water to gurgle through the ship's bottom unchecked. The black gang worked continuously below deck, but as fast as one pipe was connected another would burst.

The following tide succeeded only in sending breakers scudding against the steamer, damaging her upper works and straining the hull. Passengers were ushered into their staterooms and a mild form of panic broke out down in steerage.

On the following day, when the sea moderated sufficiently, rescue ships arrived and the passengers were immediately transferred. The crew remained aboard the *Great Republic* awaiting an opportunity to refloat her. From the shore she appeared to be virtually undamaged but the elements took only two days to begin their destruction.

The most authoritative account of the wreck was given by Captain James Carroll, the ship's master, who testified at a special hearing following the loss of the ship. Testifying that he had placed the vessel in charge of pilot Thomas Doig at 12:30 a.m. on April 19, he made the following remarks:

"There was not a ripple on the water, and we came over the bar under a slow bell all the way, crossing safely and reaching the inside buoy. The first and the third officers were on the lookout with me. I had a pair of glasses and was the first to discover Sand Island, and found the bearings all right. I reported it to the pilot, who as yet had not seen it. We ran along probably two minutes, and I then told the pilot that I thought we were getting too close to the island and that he had better haul her up. He replied, I do not think we are in far enough. A minute later I said, Port your helm and put it hard over, as I think you are getting too near the island. He made no reply, but ran along for about five minutes and then put the helm hard aport, and the vessel swung up, heading toward Astoria, but the ebb tide caught her on the starboard bow and, being so near the island, sent her on the spit. She went on so lightly that few knew of the accident, but as the tide was falling we had no chance to get the vessel off that night. The next tide was a small one, and we could do nothing and as the barometer was falling, indicating a storm, I sent Mr. Peck, the purser, to Fort Canby for assistance. The tugs *Brenham* and *Canby* arrived, followed soon afterward by the *Shubrick* and the *Columbia*. With the aid of small boats the passengers were transferred to these steamers and taken to Astoria, the *Brenham* making two trips. The entire crew remained on board and I made arrangements with Captain Flavel to have three tugs there at high tide. In the meantime the crew was at work discharging coal in an effort to lighten the vessel. At 8 p.m. a southwest gale started in making a heavy sea, chopping to the southeast about midnight. Up to this time the ship was lying easy and making no water but the heavy sea prevented the tugs from rendering assistance and also drove her higher on the spit, and shortly after midnight, she began to work, breaking the steam pipes and disabling engines. The few remaining passengers were put ashore on Sand Island at 6 a.m. on Sunday and were followed by the crew, the ship commencing to break up so that it was dangerous to remain on board. The last boat left the ship at 10:30 a.m. and in getting away the steering oar broke and the boat capsized, drowning eleven of the fourteen men it contained. About the same time a heavy sea boarded the ship and carried away the staterooms on the starboard side, gutted the dining room, broke up the floor of the social hall and carried away the piano. Several seas afterward boarded her forward and carried away the starboard guard, officer's room and steerage deck, also a number of horses. I remained aboard until 5 p.m., when the pilot and I lowered a lifeboat and came ashore."

At the time of the disaster the *Great Republic* was insured for $50,000, and her cargo at an additional $25,000. She carried 1059 tons of general freight valued at $75,000. Among the cargo were twenty-seven horses and only seven managed to reach the shore after they were dumped overboard.

Thomas Doig, pilot of the *Great Republic* was called at the hearing to give his version of the disaster. Under oath he stated:

"I took charge of the ship at the automatic buoy at 12:30 a.m. It was a starlight night, and I had no doubt about keeping the course and getting in all right. After taking charge I headed her for the bar which I crossed in safety at 12:55 a.m. I kept the lead going constantly from the time I took charge, and after crossing the bar, I put the ship under a slow bell, and ran her that way until she grounded. After crossing the bar I took my course for the middle of Sand Island with a bright lookout kept. Captain Carroll reported Sand Island to me, and I answered him and said, That's all right. He then said, Port your helm, Doig: she is getting too near the island, I answered, I don't think she is far enough in from two to four minutes. About that time I sighted Sand Island and put her helm hard over, she answering her helm and coming up on her course headed east northeast; but immediately on getting her on her course she brought up on the spit with her port bilge. On her starboard quarter I had five fathoms by the lead, and the only reason I can give for the disaster is that, when I took charge of the vessel, I did not figure on the ebb being so strong. I knew the tide had been ebbing for at least an hour and a half, but had no fear as to her not having water enough, as she was drawing but seventeen feet, and I knew there was plenty of water for that draught at that stage of the tide. The ship working under a slow bell, and the ebb tide striking her on the starboard quarter, had set her down for at least a quarter or a half a mile from where I thought I was on my course. When she brought up on the spit her headway was so slow that the jar was hardly noticeable by those who were standing on deck, and both the Captain and myself thought she would go off at the next high tide."

The decision of the marine inspectors inquiry resulted in the suspension of pilot Doig's license for one year and Captain Carroll's license for six months. Upon hearing the decision, Carroll immediately appealed to the supervising inspector and had no trouble in getting the decision against him reversed.

Passengers aboard the *Great Republic* commended the able way in which Carroll had handled the complex situation after the vessel struck the sands.

The wreck was purchased by Jackson & Meyers from the underwriters, who were represented by Captain George Flavel. The salvage firm paid $3,780 for the wreck and took into partnership J. H. D. Gray, W. S. Kinney and W. S. Gibson, of Astoria, who formed the Great Republic Wrecking Company.

They set to work immediately salvaging the remaining cargo. A month later the hull aft of the walking beam crumbled into the sea and the fore and mainmast went over the side. In another ten days the walking beam and the two large paddle wheels alone remained intact. Parts of the wreckage could be seen at low tide as late as the turn of the century. The steam-

er's grave was marked on navigation charts thereafter
as Republic Spit.

The months following the loss of the *Great Republic* were both prosperous and disastrous on the Columbia River.

On the brighter side of the ledger were events like
the arrival of the steamers *Oregon* and the *State of
California,* which marked a new era in coastwise passenger travel. The newly formed Oregon Railway and
Navigation Company offered rail and sea connections
at Portland and other ports in the area. More towns
popped up along the river banks. Lumbering, fishing
and farming became large industries. Both Astoria and
Portland prospered. But the portal to world trade
through the Columbia's entrance was still a treacherous waterway about which little had been done. It
became increasingly apparent that if the Columbia was
to meet the growing demands of maritime traffic, steps
would have to be taken to improve the bar conditions.
The combination of sand and sea would have to be
challenged.

It was in this decade that plans for the construction
of a jetty passed the talking stage and became a reality.

As the years rolled by, traffic negotiating the Columbia bar was afforded greater protection but the grim
reminders of the past and present are still in existence.

British Bark *Peter Iredale*

The *Peter Iredale's* remains still protrude from the
sands as they have for nearly a half century. Located
near Fort Stevens, the old wreck was in the line of fire
from the Japanese submarine that shelled the Oregon
Coast in the early months of World War II. The
coastal blackout was in effect and the submarine fired
blindly toward the fort. The shells cleared the wreck
and landed in the open fields without inflicting any
damage. As a protection against possible invasion the

entire beach along Clatsop Spit was lined with barb
wire which was spread over the remains of the *Iredale*.

For the story of the wreck of the *Peter Iredale*, we
will have to turn back to the early years of the century.
It was at 6 a.m., on October 25, 1906, that the *Peter
Iredale*, twenty-eight days out from Salina Cruz went
ashore on Clatsop Beach, a few miles south of the jetty.
Her distress signals alerted the Point Adams lifesaving
crew who were joined by soldiers from Fort Stevens as
they moved their rescue equipment to the scene of the
wreck. After several anxious minutes the twenty men
aboard the big British bark were removed.

Captain H. Lawrence, master of the wrecked ship,
stepped out of the surf boat and dodged about the

BARK *PETER IREDALE*

fringes of the crowd that had gathered on the beach.

"You the Captain," ventured a voice from the crowd. The skipper paid no attention to the inquirer. Undaunted the figure stepped from the mob, offered the mariner a shot of whiskey, and then proceeded to tell him that he was from the Astoria newspaper and would like Captain's version of the wreck.

Lawrence sat down on a log and commenced his tale.

"I picked up the Tillamook Light at 2 a.m. and immediately called all hands to set all sails intending to stand off for the mouth of the Columbia and pick up a pilot by day. A heavy southeast wind blew and a strong current prevailed and before the vessel could be veered around, she was in the breakers and all efforts to keep her off were unavailing.

"The first shock sent the mizzen mast overboard and when she struck again, parts of other masts snapped like pipe stems. It was a miracle that none of the crew was killed by the falling masts as the ship pounded in the surf. After the crew had escaped the danger of the falling debris, all hands were summoned aft as the vessel ran up on the shelving sands with little violence. I told them to abandon ship. The Point Adams surf boat was soon alongside and took all hands quickly and safely ashore.

"That's all I have to say."

The survivors were taken to Astoria by train and turned over to the British vice-consul, P. I. Cherry, until the wreck was investigated and the insurance matters adjusted with the owners, Iredale and Porter, of Liverpool.

Following her abandonment, the *Iredale* was whipped by gales and heavy seas. She listed to port and soon became a tangled mass of wreckage. To this day the bowsprit of the big square rigger still points skyward from the rusted foc'sle head. The remainder of the ship is down to her gunnels in the sand with the hollow iron masts still lying on her rotted decks as they have for many years. The constant pounding of the surf has beaten massive holes in the forward section which will some day also crumble into the sea.

SAILING SHIP *BATTLE ABBEY*

CHAPTER FIVE

STORM

Few months in the year pass without the storm flags flying from the local weather tower off the mouth of the Columbia, warning ships of impending danger. Ugly weather is no respecter of ships and sailors, and when the barometer falls and the wind kicks up along those stretches, mariners know it's time to get out the oil skins.

Proving that the Pacific's Graveyard is a place to be feared, is an article that appeared in the Seattle Times on January 30, 1920.

"North Head, Wash.—The hurricane which yesterday swept over this section was by far the most severe storm that ever visited the North Pacific, based upon wind velocity which according to the official weather estimates attained the speed of 160 miles per hour.

46

"According to records here, no such wind velocity has ever been reported anywhere.

"The anemometer tower at the weather station was razed by the gale after government instruments had recorded a wind of 132 miles per hour. All moveable things in the path of the storm were swept away and damage to government buildings and property was large.

"When the hurricane was at its height the government wireless antennae was blown away and the cottage which housed the family of the operator in charge was demolished. All telegraph and telephone lines were swept away and roofs of all buildings on North Head were razed and blown away. Fully eighty percent of all matured trees on North Head were razed and all roads were blocked by fallen trees and debris."

Both the Columbia and Willapa bars are extremely dangerous to navigation when the gale spreads its wrath upon their waters.

Steamer *General Warren*

Forty-two lives were sacrificed in the tragic loss of the steamer *General Warren* on Clatsop Spit, January 28, 1852. The vessel departed Portland with fifty-two persons aboard and a capacity load of grain. A long trail of black smoke belched from her stack, as the "steam kettle" moved down river leaving a frothy wake behind. Folks gathered at the river settlements to watch the vessel pass by, for in that early day steamboats were still a novelty.

Formerly a Bangor packet steamer, the *General Warren* was artistically furnished. Her main lounge presented an array of carved woodwork and plush furniture, and at the top of the grand staircase hung a life size portrait of the general for whom she was named.

Captain Flavel piloted the steamer down the river

and across the bar on what was to be her final trip. After he was picked up by the pilot schooner *Mary Taylor,* her master, Captain Charles Thompson assumed command and pointed the vessel's prow to the southwest in late afternoon on January 28. Under an overcast sky she moved slowly under steam and a light spread of canvas, but towards evening the wind had reached gale-like proportions and the foretopmast was carried away. Water seeped into the hold soaking the grain and choking the pumps.

Captain Thompson stood on the bridge maintaining his vigil all through the night. When darkness faded the vessel was put about with great difficulty and her course set for returning to the Columbia. Signal flags called for a pilot to come out and guide the vessel into calm waters, but it was 3 p.m. the following day before the pilot schooner could battle her way across the bar and put pilot Flavel aboard again.

Toward evening a strong ebb tide was running on the bar and the swells were mountainous. Flavel was not willing to make the crossing until the conditions improved, but the frightened passengers gathered around him and pleaded for him to change his decision for fear that the vessel might founder. Later came threats and shaking fists but the pilot still refused. Even the ship's master desired to risk the crossing and told Flavel that his vessel was incapable of staying afloat much longer. Again the passengers moved in on the pilot taunting him with cowardice.

In desperation Flavel mumbled, "Very well, if you insist in going I will take you in, but I refuse to be responsible for what might happen."

He signalled the pilot schooner to accompany the *Warren,* but the wind changed and the schooner drifted away from the steamer.

The vessel made little headway and water was gaining rapidly in her holds. The pilot ordered the anchors dropped, but Thompson insisted that his ship should be beached immediately if it were to be saved. Respecting the Captain's desire the course was altered and the steamer was run hard aground on the spit at 7 p.m.

All hands huddled forward. Some prayed, some cursed and others sang to keep fear from gripping them as the seas buffeted the vessel without mercy.

The ship was breaking up fast and most of the lifeboats had been demolished by the seas. Finally Thompson called for volunteers to man an undamaged lifeboat and go in search of help. There followed a long pause, for each felt his chances of survival would be better by remaining with the steamer. Finally ten men stepped forward.

With the pilot's superior knowledge of the bar, Thompson requested that he take charge of the boat. Flavel agreed, and the craft was put over the side, nothing short of a miracle keeping it from swamping.

As the feeble cheering from the passengers on the steamer faded in the distance, the men pulled the oars until across the bar. With the aid of the tide they made a remarkable run to Astoria in less than three hours. They came alongside the bark *George and Martha* at anchor in the harbor, and persuaded Captain C. Beard, master of the vessel, to send a boat to aid the shipwrecked victims.

Immediately a large whaleboat was provisioned and set out with a fresh crew to find the wreck. Fighting against odds the boat finally reached the reported scene of the stranding but nothing was visible. The *Warren* had been leveled by the tireless surf and forty-two persons were missing. The only vestige of the steamer were a few pieces of wreckage scattered along the beach.

The following day the shore was combed in the hope of finding some of the survivors, but instead only dead bodies floated in with the tide. Among them was that of Captain Thompson.

The tragic tale was climaxed with the discovery of a young married couple found dead on the beach, hands tightly locked. Her wedding ring still remained on her finger; even death could not part them.

Steamer *U. S. Grant*

On the banks of the Willamette, at a river vantage point known as Brooklyn, a suburb of East Portland, one of the Pacific Northwest's early propeller steamboats was constructed. She was launched in 1865, amid the fanfare of a group of farmers. Strange indeed, her builder was a farmer by trade, named Clinton Kelly, and his one secret ambition had always been to build a steamboat. He named his ambition *U. S. Grant*.

Competition was heavy on the upper Columbia and lower Willamette rivers, but the field was yet green down river, so off went the *Grant* to establish the first regular passenger and freight service between Astoria and Bakers Bay. The business was seasonal however, and the vessel did a variety of jobs up and down the Columbia, carrying the mails and occasionally towing a vessel across the bar. Later she became the summer tourist boat between Astoria and Ilwaco, gateway to the ocean beaches.

On the winter day of December 19, 1871, the *Grant* was berthed alongside the wharf at Fort Canby. Under wind-whipped rain the little steamer strained at her mooring lines. Only Captain J. H. D. Gray and his brother, A. W. Gray, the vessel's owners, were aboard.

They were below greasing the engine, when suddenly they became aware that the vessel had gone adrift. Nobody was on the wharf and the steamer was carried away unnoticed. The two men tried to get up steam but the boilers were cold and the ship was drifting at an alarming rate towards Sand Island. They ran forward to drop the anchors, but the powerful wind soon put the steamer on the sands.

Hastily a boat was put over the side and the two men tumbled into it before the surf could smash it to pieces. Unable to land in the surf, the boat drifted in the fury of the storm all through the night. The following day the two men were discovered huddled together in the boat, nearly frozen to death. They were picked up and brought ashore, and in spite of their experience lived for many years afterwards.

The *Grant* proved a total loss and her bones cluttered the beach for several months before the tide washed them out to sea. Her name board was hung on the wall of the Fort Canby Lifesaving Station where it remained for many years among the relics of other shipwrecks.

British Bark *Lupatia*

Having once served as a lighthouse keeper on historic Tillamook Rock, the author has heard the story of the *Lupatia* told many times by the retired lightkeepers.

The tale could well be entitled, "The Portrait of a Dog," for the only survivor of the wreck was a small Australian terrier.

As told by the late Captain H. S. Wheeler, superintendent of the lighthouse construction on Tillamook Rock:

"The weather was nasty and a strong southeast wind was blowing on January 2, 1881. At 8 p.m. the lighthouse crew heard loud voices which penetrated the darkness in ghostly fashion. One stood out above the others, shouting the strident command, 'Hard aport.' "

Realizing that a ship must be in trouble near the rock, Wheeler ordered lanterns lighted and a blazing fire built to warn the seafarers of their dangerous position.

As the wind fanned the fire in the black night, the image of a great sailing ship appeared through the murk, less than 600 feet away from the rock. For a few moments the ship's port light was visible and Wheeler was of the opinion that the vessel had heeded the warning and had stood out to sea.

When dawn broke the construction crew scanned the mile and a half between the rock and the shore and there silhouetted against dour-faced Tillamook Head was a mizzen topmost jutting from the sea. It was then that Wheeler realized that the ship had not heeded the warning but had crashed into the rocks.

Searching parties later found five thinly clad dead men in a rocky cove near the cliff, and a half mile further down the beach located another group of seven in a similar condition.

It was surmised that the men had either stripped off their clothes in attempting to swim to land or were asleep when the vessel struck and were swept into the swirling eddies and carried ashore.

When the disaster occurred the *Lupatia* was enroute to the Columbia River in ballast from Hiogo, Japan, having commenced her voyage at Antwerp. She was in command of her first officer, B. H. Raven, his brother, Captain Irvine Raven having died at sea nine days out of Antwerp. The Captain's wife was aboard at the start of the voyage but had left the ship in Japan.

When the searching party returned to the beach to give the bodies proper burial they found a shabby dog, his eyes swollen shut from the salt water. Whining incessantly and shivering with the cold the year-old animal was the sole survivor of the wreck. The dog was sent to a friend of Raven, residing at Astoria, and became the pet of its new owner.

The twelve men of the *Lupatia's* crew were carried a mile and a half inland and buried. Four other crew members reported to have been aboard the ship were never found. In the aftermath of the tragedy, Captain Wheeler ventured his theory for the loss of the *Lupatia*. He claimed that the weather was too thick to take bearings and that if the ship's master had been going by dead reckoning, the compass may have been effected by the near proximity of the shore.

The *Lupatia* was reported to have been sighted off the mouth of the Columbia the day prior to the wreck by the British bark *Dovenby*, whose master claimed that all appeared well aboard the vessel.

British Ship *Strathblane*

A row of tombstones now entwined in undergrowth at the Ilwaco cemetery is a worn reminder of the lives lost in the wreck of the British ship *Strathblane*, November 3, 1891.

Captain George Cuthell, master of the vessel, cupped his hands to his lips and called to first officer J. D. Murray in charge of the lifeboat as it pulled away from the wreck.

SCHOONER *STRATHBLANE*

"Give my love to my wife and family back home," he said. Then after a slight pause, he continued, "I suppose this will be put down as just another case of reckless navigation, but God knows, I did the best I could."

On November 2, the log book entry read: "thick fog, barometer falling fast, course Northeast by east, 19 days out from Honolulu for the Columbia River, crew employed reefing sails and all pumps attended to."

Unaware that he had been navigating with an erratic chronometer, Cuthell had figured his position to be sixty miles off shore at the time the vessel struck the beach. The weather had been so thick that it was impossible to take observations.

After the first lifeboat had left the *Strathblane,* the remaining boats were stove in by the seas and one of the frightened seamen flung himself into the surf and attempted to gain the shore, but was drowned in the attempt.

Hundreds of people gathered on the beach to watch rescue operations. The lifesaving crew from Klipsan arrived on the scene and made desperate attempts to reach the remaining seamen but each lifeline that they fired fell short of its mark. Continual attempts to launch a surf boat were made but all were repelled in the angry surf.

The seas became a tangled mass of wreckage as the *Strathblane* broke up. Those still aboard the wreck made one final attempt to reach shore after repairing the ship's damaged launch. Ten feet from the side of the ship however the craft capsized drowning all hands.

Captain Cuthell, who had elected to remain with his ship, kept his post until the decks buckled beneath his feet, waiting till all hope of saving his ship was gone, and then true to the law of the sea went down with his ship.

When the fury of the storm had abated, six bodies were washed ashore, including Cuthell's. The dead were buried in the Ilwaco cemetery, where local residents placed flowers on their graves for many years. The body of the seventh casualty was never recovered.

The *Strathblane* struck the beach on the ebb tide at 5 a.m. and had completely disintegrated by 3 p.m. the following afternoon.

For many years prior to the wreck, the *Strathblane* had operated between the United Kingdom and Portland, as a unit of the grain fleet. She first entered the river in 1878, and was one of the best known vessels in the trade.

American Schooner *Frank W. Howe*

The wrath of a southwest gale was responsible for the loss of the schooner *Frank W. Howe*, which was enroute to San Pedro from Ballard with a cargo of railroad ties in 1904.

The first news of the *Howe* in distress was received at 10 a.m. at the North Head Lighthouse when flares were sighted directly west of the station. Word was relayed to the lifesaving stations, and both the Fort Canby and Klipsan crews were directed to the beach.

Out beyond the surf a waterlogged schooner moved toward the shore. The surf was too high to launch a boat, and the lifesaving crews patiently waited for the vessel to strike the sands before attempting a rescue. Finally she struck, and immediately two line-throwing guns were set up on the sands. After several futile attempts, three lines hit their mark and a few hours later Captain A. Keegan and six crew members came ashore by breeches buoy.

"Thank God, it's all over," choked the ship's master bundling up in a warm blanket.

"We left Ballard on February 12, and all went well till the afternoon of Thursday last. We were off Yaquina Bay, about 1:30 p.m. when the vessel suddenly filled. A strong southwest gale was blowing at the time and the seas were mountain high. Since then the schooner had been waterlogged and all that kept it afloat was the cargo in her hold. We had lived in the rigging and on the deck since that time without a wink of sleep and almost nothing to eat. Realizing our desperate condition, I determined to reach the Columbia River or Cape Flattery, if possible. Sail was set and we sailed and drifted before the gale until we were off the Columbia River. About 10 a.m. on the morning of February 22, the schooner's back broke clear across under the hatch. I could not enter the Columbia, and finding the schooner would weather Cape Disappointment, I headed her for a sandy beach in order to save the lives of the balance of the crew. During the terrible ordeal a Norwegian seaman was swept from the rigging and drowned in the seas, and the cook while taking his trick at the wheel was crushed to death by a massive wall of water that cleaned the deck."

The *Frank Howe* became a total loss. She was owned at Boston, and was valued at $35,000.

American Schooner *C. A. Klose*

On the night of March 26, 1905, a derelict drifted on the beach ten miles north of Fort Canby, on North Beach Peninsula. Discovered the following day by beach dwellers, the vessel was the immediate subject of speculation.

The deserted hull came on the beach bottom up and all theory led to the belief that the entire crew had been drowned. When the tide receded the name *C. A. Klose* was plainly visible in black letters across the vessel's stern.

Checking with the pilot station at Astoria, it was learned that the vessel had passed over the Columbia bar several weeks earlier bound for San Francisco from

Vancouver, Washington, in command of Captain Nicholas Wagner.

Later reports revealed that the hulk had been sighted adrift by the tug *Dauntless* off the mouth of the Columbia before the wreck was washed up on the beach. The tug was unable to approach the derelict due to the heavy seas. On the same day the lookout at Cape Disappointment sighted the vessel but by the time his report was relayed to Astoria, it was dusk and the sea was so heavy that no tug was willing to go out after it.

Early in the morning two bar tugs started out after the hulk but were summoned back upon learning that the wreck had drifted ashore on North Beach.

The fate of the crew remained a mystery for several weeks and after all hope had been abandoned for their safety, word was received at Astoria that they had taken to the boats several miles southwest of the Columbia River, on March 21, after their ship had given indications of foundering. Later they were picked up by a southbound vessel and their whereabouts was not learned till the rescue ship made port several days later.

American Schooner *Admiral*

While homebound from Valparaiso for Grays Harbor, the four-masted schooner *Admiral* finished her career, January 13, 1912, after striking the south jetty of the Columbia bar in a gale that drove her sixty miles off her course.

It was nearly eight bells when the telephone on the wall of the Point Adams Lifesaving Station rang. Captain O. S. Wicklund, officer in charge, answered the call and heard the voice of the keeper from one of the neighboring light stations.

"I received a wireless message from a tanker this morning stating that a four-masted schooner was in trouble off the south jetty," said the voice.

Outside the weather was bitter and the rain slanted down from the gray clouds hanging low over the mouth of the river.

Clicking up the telephone receiver, Wicklund alerted the life-saving crew and then called the wireless station for any additional information, but to his dismay found that the wires had blown down.

The bar was impassable, and accordingly he made arrangements to go to Fort Stevens and run the steam locomotive, used for repairing the jetty, out to the ship. With communications damaged Wicklund set out on foot for the fort, bucking the wind and rain for three miles until he had reached his destination. Both the engineer and fireman who operated the locomotive volunteered to aid in the rescue, and after getting up steam, started down the track. In the terrific wind and high seas there was danger that the trestle had been carried away. The accompanying fog all but obliterated the track from view. As the engine crept along at a snail's pace, all eyes were strained ahead.

Suddenly on the track ahead the engineer sighted the dim outline of a uniformed man carrying a bundle. The figure was down on his hands and knees slowly crawling. The engine jerked to a stop and the three men jumped out of the cab to aid the man who later identified himself as Captain Joseph Bender of the schooner *Admiral*. The bundle in his arms was his infant child which he held close to his body to keep it from freezing.

Gasping for breath, the captain pointed down the track. "My wife! My wife!" he said, "Go get my wife."

A few feet further the engine clanked to a halt again and there was the Captain's wife clad in a thin nightgown which revealed her youthful form. Wicklund picked her up and carried her back to the cab where she fainted after asking for her baby.

A hundred feet farther the ship's cook was found on the trestle.

With the cab filled, the little engine back-tracked three miles to get medical aid for the survivors at Fort Stevens.

When the locomotive arrived, the lifesaving crew was waiting with the breeches buoy and line-throwing gun which they had loaded on a flatcar. The engine was connected up and started across the trestle with the lifesaving crew and their gear.

Before the engine left on its second trip, Captain Bender told Wicklund that the schooner had been carried into the jetty, and that he believed that the trestle had been smashed somewhere along the line. Thus caution was exercised to prevent the locomotive from plunging into the sea.

Passing the three-mile mark, the gap was sighted, and not only was the trestle smashed, but a 200-foot gap of open water separated the two segments of the jetty.

At the opposite side of the break, the murk lifted sufficiently to sight the remainder of the shipwrecked sailors. With accuracy a line was fired across the gap and made fast, and one by one the shivering survivors were brought to safety.

All hands were accounted for, but the schooner was nowhere in the locality. Later it was learned that the seventy-mile wind and heavy seas had driven the *Admiral* over top of the rock strewn jetty into the channel where it drifted with the currents towards Peacock Spit. The bar tug *Wallula* attempted to salvage the schooner after three members of the tug's crew had boarded the wreck to make a tow line secure. While pulling the line aboard, the schooner capsized and the three men were thrown into the sea and nearly drowned. The vessel was carried onto the spit where it broke up shortly after.

The *Admiral* was owned by the Pacific Shipping Company of San Francisco at the time of her loss, and had been engaged in various Pacific trade lanes since her building at North Bend, Oregon, in 1899.

British Bark *Melanope*

On a bright morning in December, 1906, a curious looking craft floated into the prevailing currents several miles off the Columbia. A lookout perched in the crow's nest of the steamer *Northland* was scanning the horizon when his glasses fell upon the strange appearing craft. After a critical examination he scrambled down the ladder to announce his find. In a few moments a boat was swung over the side and its crew pulled toward the reported location.

Fifteen minutes later details of the craft began to show more clearly. There was no sign of life aboard; her spars were dangling in the fittings and the masts broken at the hounds. The hull bore a color of brown and dingy gray, which as they drew near showed as iron rust. Under the shattered bowsprit projected the weather-worn figurehead representing a god of the sea. The vessel strained under a severe starboard list. Aft on the starboard quarter were iron davits with blocks intact—but no falls and no boat. On the port quarter a boat still rocked to and fro. In the deadeyes in the channels could be seen frayed rope-yarns and ragged sails draped here and there on the slanting decks.

As the boat rounded the stern of the derelict the crew read in raised letters, flecked here and there, the name *Melanope*. Badly mauled by the storm, the vessel had come in from the mysterious sea to tell her story.

The seamen from the steamer climbed the channels, fastened the painter and peered over the rails. Only the creaking of the loose tackle filled their ears.

Then from the foc'sle came a strange cry and the

men worked their way forward and crept into the dank quarters. There sat a small dog nearly starved to death. He was the only living thing aboard the derelict. What had happened to the crew?

Eyeing the prospects of salvage, the *Northland* took the wreck in tow, and after encountering considerable trouble bringing her over the bar, finally got the derelict to Astoria, where it was pumped out and eventually sold to Captain James Griffiths, through her operators, J. J. Moore & Company, of San Francisco. Her new owner cut the vessel down to a barge.

Several weeks later it was learned that the *Melanope's* crew had hurriedly abandoned the ship after it was dismasted in a gale and thrown over on its beam ends. They left in such a rush that they forgot the little dog who was the ship's mascot.

The master of the *Melanope*, Captain N. K. Wills,, expressed amazement when he heard that his vessel had not foundered, and also that the little dog had weathered the ordeal.

Sailors who at one time or another had shipped out in the *Melanope* pointed to the incident as just another in the life of a ship that had had a curse placed upon it.

On the *Melanope's* maiden voyage from England in 1876, she stood out to sea under the banner of Potter & Company of Liverpool. She was bound for Australia well freighted in addition to a large passenger list. Before the tug had cast off, an old woman resembling a witch was discovered peddling apples to the passengers. Nobody on board knew where she had come from.

When Captain Watson discovered the woman he ordered her to leave his ship at once. The action so infuriated her that she blasphemed him with language that would have surpassed the devil himself. It took three burly seamen to control the screaming, clawing apple peddler, as they handed her down to the tug, while the passengers looked on in amusement.

From the deck of the tug, the woman yelled, "I curse you ship *Melanope*, for as long as you shall sail the seas," and then she shook her fist at Captain Watson as the tug steamed back to port.

Sailors of old never treated a curse lightly. It was without precedent that the *Melanope* was dismasted in a gale on her initial voyage, and in subsequent passages met with other troubles. On one occasion her master ran away with an Indian princess, who drank herself to death after tireless days at sea. Shortly after, the captain went insane and threw himself to the sharks. The mate took charge of the vessel and landed the crew at San Francisco penniless. The ship had to be sold to pay them off. One of the seamen complained that he had seen the mate counting gold coins which he had stolen from the Captain's cabin after he was drowned.

Then came the incident off the Columbia River and finally her role as a barge. The old iron hull which now resembles an old witch of the sea, is still afloat in 1950, in Canadian waters.

American Tanker *Rosecrans*

In the year 1913, three ships were lost in the Pacific's Graveyard.

The most tragic was the loss of the tanker *Rosecrans,* which plunged to the bottom off Peacock Spit, taking the lives of thirty-three. Only two survivors were removed from the wreckage.

If ever a luckless vessel sailed the seas, it was the *Rosecrans,* launched at Glasgow, Scotland, in 1884, as the *Methven Castle,* of the Union Castle Line. A few years later she was sold and renamed *Columbia,* and eventually came under American registry.

During the Spanish American War, the ship joined

the United States Army as the transport *Rosecrans,* but so displeased was the military with her high operating costs, that she was disposed of shortly after.

Next the *Rosecrans* came to the Pacific Coast to be converted from a troop ship to a tanker for the Associated Oil Company, of San Francisco.

On March 12, 1912, after fighting a furious gale off the California Coast she became unmanageable and was tossed broadside on the rocks at Alcatraz, twenty-two miles north of Santa Barbara. Two crew members were drowned. After being abandoned to the underwriters, the Whitelaw Salvage Company performed an amazing salvage job and ushered the tanker off to San Francisco to patch up a twenty-five foot hole in her hull.

Six months later the *Rosecrans* was completely gutted by fire while loading oil at Gaviota, but again her hull was salvaged and rebuilt at a tremendous cost.

Captain L. F. Johnson was her master during both mishaps, and the same skipper was in command when the vessel was lost for good on the morning of January 7, 1913, at the mouth of the Columbia.

The *Rosecrans* was enroute to Portland from San Francisco with 20,000 barrels of crude oil valued at $200,000 when she sailed into a sixty mile gale off the mouth of the Columbia River. Captain Johnson lost his bearings, and let his ship over-run the channel entrance and came head on with the tip of Peacock Spit.

A distress message was picked up at Cape Disappointment at 5:15 a.m.

"Steamer *Rosecrans* on bar, send assistance, ship breaking up fast; can stay at my station no longer."

Then everything went silent and the race against death was on. By 8 a.m. the tanker broke in two and the crew was forced into the rigging for safety from the angry sea. One by one they gave up the struggle and were swept into the boiling surf. Finally only three remained, and the mast to which they clung was all that rose above the surface.

Under the most hazardous conditions a surf boat from Point Adams reached the wreck. As the boat maneuvered near the mast one of the three survivors became overly anxious and threw himself in the water in an effort to reach the rescuers, but before his exhausted body was pulled aboard, he had drowned. The other two were rescued.

So rough was the bar that the boat was unable to make the return crossing and, after several hours, the shore stations gave it up as lost in the tempest. Instead the boat reached the lightship and all hands were taken safely aboard. While attempting to lift the surfboat on the deck of the lightship, the lines parted and it went adrift still bearing the lifeless body of the seaman who had flung himself from the mast.

It wasn't until two days later that the tug *Oneonta* made her way across the bar and picked up the survivors on the lightship.

Upon reaching Astoria, the two survivors Erick Lindmark, ship's carpenter, and Joseph Stenning, quartermaster, both claimed that Captain Johnson had mistaken the lightship for North Head, and had never regained his bearings. Shortly after, the vessel struck the spit.

Meanwhile, the nation's newspapers screamed headlines telling of the disaster, one of the worst of the year.

American Steam Schooner *Caoba*

On the beach five miles north of Ocean Park, lies a rust-riddled boiler, the last remembrance of the steam schooner *Caoba*, cast ashore February 5, 1925, in a severe blow.

Outbound from Willapa Bay laden with lumber the

Caoba ran into a sudden gale of such velocity that her 400 horsepower engine was incapable of making any headway. Laboring under her twenty years and a heavy deckload, the steamer developed a most unholy appetite for salt water. She spat all the oakum from her seams and all hands could note the course she made by merely watching the track of spent oakum astern. Three or four feet of bilge wash was nothing to worry about but when it rose to nine feet despite the efforts of all hands pumping, it was time to make quick decisions.

The water put out the boiler fires and the vessel appeared to be afloat by the deckload, which gave indications of popping the gripes under the strain.

"All hands man the lifeboats," barked Captain Alfred Sandvig, "It's black and stormy out there, but we'll take our chances."

Two boats put out into the heaving sea, and for thirty-eight hours were tossed about like matchsticks. By morning they had drifted apart; the first boat was

STEAM SCHOONER *CAOBA*

found by the tug *John Cudahy,* but the other was listed as missing with ten souls. Then from out of the misty dawn appeared a ship, and it turned out to be a Canadian rumrunner, named the *Pescawha,* commanded by Captain R. Pamphley.

The grateful survivors were taken aboard, suffering intensely from the cold, but what the Canadian ship carried soon warmed their spirits.

Before the crew of the *Caoba* could be landed, the *Pescawha* unfortunately fell in company with the Coast Guard cutter *Algonquin,* which promptly seized the vessel for carrying liquor inside the limits of the United States boundaries. The government vessel ran down the *Pescawha* and towed her back to Astoria with some 1200 cases of liquor stacked in her holds. When the vessel was docked, her officers were immediately placed under arrest and a guard put around the vessel. It was believed that three-quarters of the cargo was dumped before the vessel was seized.

The Coast Guard was bitterly assailed in the press by those who felt strongly that traditions of the sea had been observed by the crew of the rumrunner in rescuing the seamen and that they should not have been interned. As a result of the seizure, however, twenty-three shore operators of the bootleg enterprise were picked up and convicted.

U. S. Customs Inspector Harry J. Strowbridge took over the *Pescawha* in Astoria. The cargo was discharged at the dockside and reloaded again for evidence in Portland. During the stevedoring operations, twenty-seven cases of liquor were found missing.

Meanwhile the *Caoba,* held afloat by her cargo of lumber, was driven ashore near Ocean Park, on February 5. Her wooden hull lay on the beach for many years and gradually disappeared until only her rusted boiler remained to break the level contour of the acres of sand.

Sudden & Christenson, of San Francisco, were the owners of the *Caoba*.

American Motor Vessel *Pescawha*

After her brush with the law the *Pescawha* became a black sheep among seafarers. She was sold and re-sold and spent much of her time straining at her lines for another chance to go back to sea.

The scene takes place eight years after her capture by the *Algonquin*. The *Pescawha* now had the American flag flying from her staff, and had become a re-formed unit of illegal trades. She shoved off from her berth on what was to be her last voyage. The date was February 27, 1933, and the scene was on the lower Columbia.

The *Pescawha* a few months earlier had been sold to an adventurer who proceeded to interest a party of ten young men in what was said to be a whaling expedition. The vessel was fitted with special gear and equipment for capturing and rendering whales.

Her crew of amateur mechanics installed a balky Maxwell car engine on the deck, where they could administer to its humors. A makeshift belt transmitted power to the propeller.

Despite the fact that a southwester was blowing, the *Pascawha* put out to sea, her sails clewed down and the Maxwell purring. Her course was down the middle of the channel. She should have hugged the south edge of the waterway to allow for drift in the port tack.

The Maxwell faltered and died off buoy No. 10, and the set of the ebb tide put the vessel into the north jetty. Her skipper was crushed against the housing as the lifeboat was knocked from the davits while the crew was attempting to put it over the side.

The other crew members survived, reaching the jetty on debris. Their escape was regarded as remark-able for the ebb was sweeping along the huge boulders of the jetty with considerable force. The *Pescawha* was reduced to splinters with the wheel being the largest piece of wreckage found by the beachcombers.

The body of the skipper, Captain Victor H. Riley, of Oregon City, was recovered in Deadman's Cove.

When gray dawn broke over the bar, the *Pescawha* was no more, and there off the jetty her pranks of dodging the law, and her attempts at reformation had their closing chapter.

American Freighter *Laurel*

The eyes and ears of the world were on a "die hard" ship master who refused to abandon his ship after it had broken in two and was given up as a total loss. His tenacity in remaining with his ship afforded front page newspaper material, but his role as a hero angered the Coast Guard.

It all came about in a howling southwester when the Quaker Line operated freighter *Laurel* was outbound across the Columbia bar with seven million

STEAMSHIP *LAUREL*

feet of lumber destined for New York and Philadelphia, on June 16, 1929.

As the high seas buffeted the ship, the steering engine became disabled and she was swept on Peacock
Spit. Mammoth breakers pounded the vessel unmerci-
fully and calls of distress crackled over the wireless
asking immediate assistance.

The Coast Guard managed to get a boat over the
bar but it was unable to approach the stranded ship.
The deckload had been carried overboard and the surf
was a solid mass of lumber. In early morning the
steamship broke in two just forward the bridge and a
nineteen year old seaman named Russell Smith was
carried to his death. The thirty-two other crew members gathered on the after half of the vessel to await
rescue.

By this time the cutter *Redwing* was standing off the
wreck waiting to pick up the survivors should the
lifeboats manage to navigate through the lumber-laden
sea. After several futile attempts the lifeboats worked
in near the after section of the *Laurel* and managed to
remove twenty-four shipwrecked seamen, but were
unable to save those remaining until the following
day, when the seas had moderated.

While the rescue work continued, word was received
that the steam schooner *Multnomah* was in trouble on
the bar. It was reported that she had lost 600,000 feet
of lumber from her deckload after boiler trouble had
been encountered. Torn between two rescue missions,
the Coast Guard dispatched the pilot schooner to go
to the aid of the *Multnomah*. Fifteen passengers were
removed from the steam schooner, but shortly after
they were evacuated, temporary repairs were made on
the ship's boiler and the Coast Gaurd was relieved to
learn that the vessel had reached Astoria under it's own
power.

Turning their efforts back to the *Laurel*, Coastguardsmen rescued all hands, with the exception of Captain Louis Johnson, master, who refused to leave his ship despite pleas by the rescue crew. The *Redwing* finally shoved off for Astoria to get medical aid for some of the survivors.

From Cape Disappointment, a steady watch was maintained over the freighter as the crashing seas licked at her remains. Planes flew over the ship and snapped pictures of the skipper pacing the deck in defiance of the conquering elements. For fifty-four hours he remained on the bridge as another gale hammered the ship, placing his life in grave peril. As the swells rolled across the bar, the forward section of the wreck was carried fully 800 feet from the after half of the freighter.

When hope was about to be abandoned for Johnson's life, a white flag suddenly appeared on the ship's bridge indicating that he was ready to come ashore.

Several hours later the motor lifeboat fought its way to the side of the wreck, and the Captain, bearing the ship's papers, money and a few personal belongings, slid down a manila rope to the rescue craft.

Upon reaching shore Johnson was quizzed concerning his refusal to abandon the ship several hours earlier.

"I didn't want to be a hero," he smiled, "I stayed on what was left of the ship to protect it's cargo from salvagers. I had hoped that the after section of the ship would be washed on the beach so salvage would be possible, but the bulkheads gave away which prompted me to fly the white flag."

He had kept a fire going the entire time he was aboard the wreck and had sufficient food and water to last him indefinitely.

So ended the story of a ship master's vigil and the life of a freighter.

American Freighter *Iowa*

Peacock Spit claimed the freighter *Iowa* and her entire complement of thirty-four men January 12, 1936. The tragedy was one of the blackest marks against the Columbia River bar.

The vessel, owned by the States Steamship Company, was outbound from the river when a gale estimated to have had a velocity of seventy-six miles per hour, struck. The steamer crossed the bar shortly after midnight and fought against the gale until she was swept on Peacock Spit, early Sunday morning.

Only one faint S.O.S. message emanated from the *Iowa's* wireless room, but that was enough to get the Coast Guard cutter *Onondaga* underway. The cutter experienced the worst the bar could offer before it finally came in sight of the wreck. Only the *Iowa's* masts and samson posts were above the sea and all signs of life had vanished. Massive whirlpools swished around the grave of the ship.

STEAMSHIP *IOWA*

No survivors, no solution! Nobody will ever know the direct cause that led to the loss of the *Iowa* because dead men tell no tales. Competent authorities surmised that the vessel was caught broadside by the gale's fury and carried from her course in the main channel through loss of steerage, either by a damaged rudder or injury to her steering engine.

The *Iowa* was commanded by Captain Edgar L. Yates, veteran ship master, who was familiar with the Columbia bar, having piloted many ships across its reaches during his seafaring career.

For days after the wreck the beaches were strewn with oil smeared lumber, sacks of flour, rope, shingles, matches and a hundred other items which had been loaded on Puget Sound and at Longview her final port of departure. Among the wreckage only six bodies were recovered.

From the sailors union hall in Portland came a storm of protests demanding an immediate investigation as to why the *Iowa* had crossed the bar in the face of a fierce gale. The wreck was probed, but evidence was lacking. The ship was resting in Davey Jones' Locker, and there were no witnesses.

American Steam Schooner *Trinidad*

On May 7, 1937, one of the most widely heralded rescues of the north Pacific took place off Willapa bar when the steam schooner *Trinidad* stretched her ribs across the sands.

The *Trinidad* was outbound from Willapa Bay with a load of lumber for San Francisco merchants. Head on into a sixty-mile gale went the vessel staggering like a drunken man. Like the rest of the wooden lumber fleet, her flexible hull had yawning seams, and her master would have bet on a stack of holystones that his crew had pumped the entire north Pacific through her hull twice.

Her departure port of Raymond lay astern and only the Pacific's fury was ahead, but the ship had crossed the bar and for several hours had tried in vain to outwit the gale. She retreated under the strain and was driven hard on a submerged shoal off North Spit, a mile due west of Willapa Light, between buoys 6 and 7.

There was a crash of splintering wood which shivered the vessel from stem to stern as snapping gripes loosened the deckload and sent it sprawling. Timbers struck end on or broadside to, smashing and tearing. The crew gathered on the bridge as Captain I. Hellestone, pondered the fate of his ship and crew.

Elsewhere on the scene, the Willapa Bay motor lifeboat was out on the Pacific aiding a distressed fish boat and when the lookout at the tower sighted flares from the spit at 8:15 p.m., there was nothing to do but summon help from the Coast Guard at the Westport Station on Grays Harbor.

At the height of the gale, the Grays Harbor boat immediately got underway. Five men in a thirty-six

STEAM SCHOONER *TRINIDAD*

foot motor lifeboat started down the coast with H. J. Perssons, the boatswain, in charge.

For fourteen miles lifeboat *"3829"* battled walls of water, shaking herself like a wet poodle and going back for more. About 3 a.m., Perssons was greatly relieved to sight a flare from the otherwise black night. The wreck had been found at last.

The lifeboat maneuvered in close to the *Trinidad*. Each breaker brought with it the power to crush the lifeboat against the side of the wreck, but by moving in at the opportune time and pulling out with each swell, the lifeboat somehow managed to remove twenty-one crew members from the bridge. Only the second mate, Werner Kraft, was carried to his death.

For this act of heroism and ability, the crew of the *"3829"* was awarded the gold Congressional Medal for the most outstanding performance of lifesaving during the year 1937.

The luckless steam schooner had stranded so far out on the bar that she was a direct target for the full fury of the gale, which knocked her to pieces within a few hours.

Russian Freighter *Vaslav Vorovsky*

The only Russian ship ever claimed by the sands of the Columbia bar was the 374 foot steamship *Vazlav Vorovsky*, pounded to pieces after stranding on Peacock Spit, April 3, 1941, while outbound with a $1,750,000 cargo of heavy machinery for Vladivostok.

It was midnight when the Russian commenced her ill-fated voyage. As she moved toward the open Pacific, a driving forty-mile gale moved in from the south. The vessel rolled and pitched and so rough was the sea that the ship was forced back and attempted to gain calmer waters. Her steering mechanism jammed and both anchors were dropped in an effort to keep her from drifting. The anchors, however, were no match for the seas and the vessel drove on the spit, southeast of the Cape Disappointment Lighthouse.

Three motor lifeboats went to the aid of the stricken freighter and successfully removed the crew of thirty-seven, two of whom were women. The survivors were taken to the Coast Guard station at Point Adams, until arrangements could be made for them at Astoria.

The *Vorovsky's* master, Captain J. Tokareff, refused to leave his ship and signalled the lifeboat to shove off. It was known to be punishable by death for a shipmaster to lose his command under the regime of Communist Russia, and Tokareff intended to stand by until all hope was gone.

As the wind whistled across the sea, it became increasingly apparent that the vessel was in a dangerous position and was working hard on the bar. Tugs stood by the wreck, but abandoned thoughts of refloating the freighter when she began to break up.

Twenty-four hours after the stranding, Tokareff signaled the shore station with blinker light, that he was

STEAMSHIP *VAZLAV VOROVSKY*

ready to quit his ship, and the surf boat promptly went out to rescue him.

The following day the vessel folded like an accordian, with two giant cracks buckling her steel hull. One break was fully eight feet wide. The local fishermen had a holiday picking loot from the wreck but the water was too shallow for larger vessels to salvage any heavy machinery.

By the summer of 1950 only a few of the frames of the ship were visible on the low tide.

U. S. Army Ferry *Arrow*

Digging her own grave in the sands at Cranberry Road, two miles north of Long Beach, the deactivated Army ferry *Arrow* lay while Army guardsmen kept a stern eye on 1500 souvenir hunters. Such was the situation surrounding the stranding of the *Arrow* on February 13, 1947.

The vessel was under tow from Puget Sound to the Columbia River where she was to have been placed in the reserve fleet, near Tongue Point. Severe seas were encountered by the Army tug and the towing line parted twice, but each time was retrieved by the tug's crew. As the seas mounted the hawser snapped again, the *Arrow* was carried toward the shore and trapped in the surf, driving hard up on the beach.

Ideas of getting the 320 foot vessel off soon diminished as the sand hollowed out around her hull. When hopes of salvage were dismissed, the Arrow was put up for sale on an "as is, where is" basis. Several salvage companies looked over the wreck, but most of them agreed that the vessel would be completely swallowed by the sands within the period of a month.

Nobody wanted the ship and finally the Army withdrew their guards and left the Arrow to any who wished to pick at her remains. She settled deep in the sand but stayed intact until the summer of 1949, when local steel cutters removed what remained above the sands between tides. Some of the peninsula fishermen were slightly irritated for they had enjoyed fishing off her rusty fantail. The wreck had also become a first class tourist attraction.

Like great people whose success is forgotten in their sunset years so it was with the *Arrow*. Few knew she had once been a palatial luxury liner on the east coast. Built at Bath, Maine, in 1909, as the steamer *Belfast*, she had operated as a unit of the Colonial Navigation Company, of New York. Painted a brilliant white on her exterior, she had lavish appointments on the interior, which would have stood out in contrast to the dull gray paint and steel bulkheads of her latter days. Her glamorous career ended when the Army took her over, for everything on the luxurious side went by the board.

Serving the military throughout World War II, the *Arrow* was operated as an inter-island ferry in the Hawaiian Islands where her 4000 horsepower engine had churned thousands of miles carrying troops and supplies.

To keep the memory of the *Arrow* green the citizens of Ocean Park removed her masts and placed them as a war memorial at the town's entrance to the beach, which leads to the twenty-eight-mile-long peninsula.

American Fish Boat *Rose Ann*

In February, 1948, the object of a wide search by the Coast Guard was the sixty-four foot fishing vessel *Rose Ann*, reported missing after departing Astoria with a crew of four men. Though planes searched a wide area and ships had been on a constant lookout, no clue to the vessels whereabouts was found. Finally the craft was given up for lost.

Two months later the dragger *Jack Junior* caught her nets on some large object in several fathoms off the mouth of the Columbia. So heavy was the object that it could not be lifted, but the position was marked.

Speculation led to the theory that the obstruction might be the steel hull of the *Rose Ann.* A few weeks later the drag boat *Princess Aho,* skippered by George Moskovita, got her net fouled in the same area and promply sent to Astoria for a diver.

Great interest was aroused as the diver descended. Instead of the *Rose Ann,* he found the object to be an ancient hand wrought anchor weighing about three tons.

The *Rose Ann* has yet to be located, but it is interesting to note that the old anchor might have been lost from one of the many wrecks that have occured off Clatsop spit. Perhaps it belonged to the *City of Dublin,* the *Edith Lorne,* the *Fern Glen* or one of the many victims of the storm.

MOTORSHIP *CHILDAR*

CHAPTER SIX

VICTORY OVER THE ELEMENTS

Seldom indeed did a ship gain her freedom once trapped on the shoals of the Pacific's Graveyard. The exceptions were a victory over the elements.

Canadian Schooner *Jenny Jones*

The schooner *Jenny Jones*, Captain James Jones, master, several days out of Victoria B. C. for Portland, stood off the mouth of the Columbia River, May 13, 1864. On board were twenty-one seasick pasengers and five crew members. The vessel carried a cargo consisting of ten casks of ale, one box of codfish, one pipe of brandy, 615 bundles of pig iron, twenty-eight crates of crockery, 200 bars of sugar and five crates of glassware.

Amid cantankerous seas, several casks of ale had

broken open and a vigorous odor permeated the schooner causing it to reek like a floating brewery.

Rolling in the trough of the seas, the vessel awaited the arrival of a pilot all day, but the bar schooner failed to appear.

Towards late afternoon of the following day the bar showed signs of moderating and Jones decided to attempt the crossing without a pilot. He chose the north channel, but when the ship was on the bar, the wind blew itself out and the schooner was left at the mercy of the currents drifting broadside into Woodpecker Spit, where the surf engulfed her.

All hands, including the passengers, were mustered at the hatches to pass up cargo and toss it overboard to lighten the vessel's burden. Seamen and landlubbers worked hand and hand for hours until at last the pilot boat appeared off the starboard quarter.

So eager were the passengers to be rescued that a boat was put over the side, swamping as soon as it hit the water and throwing four of its occupants into the surf. One by one they were dragged out, half drowned but still alive.

The pilot schooner stood near the wreck but was unable to get in near enough to rescue the party of the wrecked ship. Suddenly the *Jenny* began bumping over the reef for 1000 feet and drifted into deep water. Her stern post was stove, her fittings knocked loose and five feet of water slopped in her bilge, but, undaunted, Captain Jones, a typical sea dog, hoisted a watersoaked sail on the mainmast and got his rudderless schooner underway.

Three hours later the *Jenny* dropped her anchor off Astoria, and all hands except the skipper were removed from the vessel.

"Better get ashore and get warmed up," hollared the master of the pilot schooner.

"Hell," retorted Jones, spitting over the taffrail, "it's all in the day's work."

French Brig *Sidi*

Leaving San Francisco on February 14, 1874, the brig *Sidi* ran into a succession of dirty weather. It was not until March 1 that she arrived off the mouth of the Columbia, and her charterers, Morgan & Sons, of Portland, were greatly worried over her whereabouts.

A soupy fog hung over the river entrance, and Captain Cometoux, making his initial trip to the river, was concerned about the position of his command. Dead reckoning informed him that he was dangerously near the river opening and with an unfavorable breeze approaching, he ordered the helm hard up, and crossed the bar.

At the far end of Sand Island the wind died and the vessel was forced to drop both anchors. The currents started her dragging, and towards evening the tug *C. J. Brenham*, under Captain J. Hill, came to her aid and attempted to get a line aboard. The seas had kicked up considerably and the tug was unable to get close enough to make the line fast. At 10 p. m. the *Sidi* struck, at slack tide, and within a few hours was left high and dry on a shelf of sand. The crew walked ashore without getting their feet wet.

The following day the tug returned to investigate salvage possibilities. The stranded vessel rested in a precarious position, the tug's crew observed, but found that the underwriters were willing to sell her as she lay. Captain Hill and his crew, consisting of George Warren, George Woods and G. W. Raymond, joined forces with Captain William Koerner and F. C. Carr of Astoria, and purchased the wreck for a meager sum.

The men set to work immediately, their skill and determination motivated by the fact that the *Sidi* was insured for $50,000, and was only eight months out of the builder's shipyard. Day after day the work continued, the men divided between patching the hull and digging the sand from around the vessel. Several weeks later with the aid of a high tide, the 276 ton brig was refloated and towed to Astoria for further repairs.

The venture was a financial success and the vessel was immediately booked to carry lumber from Knappton to San Francisco. She was accepted under American registry, renamed *Sea Waif,* and sold to George Hume, shipping magnate of San Francisco.

American Steamship *Queen of the Pacific*

Averting what could have been a major disaster, the palatial passenger liner *Queen of the Pacific* was successfully refloated from Clatsop Beach in the fall of 1883.

The big steamer made her triumphant entry on the Pacific Coast in the summer of eighty-two, and Californians hailed her as she passed through the Golden Gate. Just out of the yards, her Philadelphia builders had spared nothing in making her the finest afloat. Her owners, the Pacific Coast Steamship Company, had paid a substantial amount for the liner, for competition had demanded the best.

The *Queen of the Pacific* was placed in charge of Captain Ezekiel Alexander, and entered coastwise service in the fall, arriving at Portland from San Francisco, September 18, 1882, with 300 passengers and a sizeable cargo.

The following year when destruction threatened, no efforts were spared to save the money-making liner.

It was to have been a celebrated voyage when the *Queen of the Pacific* departed San Francisco. Among her large passenger list were several members of the social world, and a collection of railroad executives enroute north to witness the driving of the famous gold spike for the completion of the Northern Pacific Railroad.

When the steamer reached the mouth of the Columbia, pilot A. D. Wass boarded from the pilot schooner, but shortly after he took command, the vessel was enshrouded in a heavy fog. She drifted from the channel range and went hard ashore on Clatsop Spit, September 5. Immediately the screws went into reverse, spinning violently, but the vessel remained fast on the sands.

When the news reached Astoria, crowds of townsfolk set out for the beach to view the liner and to watch the evacuation of 230 passengers.

A dispatch from the vessel's owners in San Francisco said that the steamer must be saved regardless of the cost.

Five of the most powerful tugs in the area were summoned for salvage work. They included the *C. J. Brenham, Astoria, Columbia, Pioneer* and the *General Miles,* all of which got lines on the stranded liner and proceeded to churn the waters. Hawsers became tight as fiddle strings, and billows of smoke belched forth from their stacks. Several hawsers were severed but the stocky tugs would go back for more punishment, and the job went on hour after hour.

Fortunately the weather conditions remained mild and the work was able to continue. Finally with the aid of a high tide the vessel loosened her grip on the sands. On the flood tide they finally got her free. The five tugs and the liner all gave prolonged blasts of their whistles and the valleys for miles around echoed the good news that the *Queen of the Pacific* had been saved.

The combined salvage force after a debated litigation were awarded $65,000 for services rendered, and the steamer continued a long and prosperous career after extensive repairs were made.

Several years later her name was shortened to *Queen,* and she was operated in the California, Puget Sound and Alaska runs. On February 27, 1904, she suffered a fire off the Oregon coast, and fourteen lives were lost before the vessel finally reached Puget Sound. The *Queen* was purchased by the Japanese in 1938, and sailed across the Pacific to be broken up for scrap.

Columbia River Lightship No. 50

Columbia River Lightship No. 50 was the first lightship stationed on the Pacific Coast. The vessel was built by the Union Iron Works of San Francisco and towed north by the tug *Fearless.* She took her station off the mouth of the Columbia River and maintained her vigil until cast ashore near McKenzie Head seven years later.

The *No. 50* was 112 feet long with a twenty-six-foot beam and a depth of twelve and one-half feet, and was constructed with steel frames and oak planking. Her heavy construction enabled her to brave the most severe weather. The stem, sternpost, keel and rudder were of steel.

Her arrival on the Columbia was received with great ceremony. Mariners recognized the lightship as a welcome and comforting sight in fair weather or foul.

The vessel was not engined and was dependent on her jury rig for propulsion. She was equipped with two horizontal return tubular boilers which furnished steam to blow a twelve-inch foghorn and to raise lights on the mast by nightfall. The night lights on her two masts consisted of six lamps placed in a circle around the crosstrees to afford visibility from any direction. By day the lamps were lowered but the vessel was easily recognized by her name painted in large letters on her sides. She was equipped with comfortable quarters for a small crew and her compartments were thoroughly watertight and seaworthy.

COLUMBIA RIVER LIGHTSHIP NO. 50

The vessel was stationed two miles south of the whistle buoy, but in 1894 was shifted further south to better facilitate ships crossing the bar.

On November 28, 1899, the *No. 50* was buffeted by terrific winds and unusually high seas which caused her to slip her anchor cables and drift toward shore in the blackness of the night.

At the crack of dawn the tugs *Escort, Wallula* and the lighthouse tender *Manzanita* raced to the side of the drifting lightship. The *Wallula* arrived first and managed to get a line on her. The tug had nearly gained the river entrance with its troublesome tow, when the hawser parted. The *Manzanita* then maneuvered in and put her line on the lightship, but it got tangled in her propeller and also broke. Next came the *Escort,* but she no sooner had begun to tow the vessel than her hawser also snapped.

Fear was felt for the eight crewmen aboard the lightship, but all rescue efforts had proved futile. The *Escort* stood by till 7 p. m. when the lightship went aground on the sands inside McKenzie Head.

When the tide receeded the *No. 50* was left high on the beach and from her position, salvage appeared a virtual impossibility. Captain Joseph Harriman and his crew were removed from the vessel, little the worse for their experiences.

The lightship remained on an even keel for several months, but her presence off the bar was badly missed and the experts were figuring some way of getting her off the sands. The solution for salvaging the lightship proved to be a unique operation.

It was determined that, because of shoals and currents, she could not be launched back into the ocean; consequently engineers of the Lighthouse Board concluded to attempt to move her across the peninsula and launch her into Bakers Bay. It was a journey of a mile, across beds of loose sand, through a forest, and over several elevations; a big job, for which there was hardly a precedent. But they got to work, jacked the vessel up out of the sand, put enormously heavy trucks under her, rigged windlasses to haul the trucks, and got stout teams of horses to turn the windlasses. At the same time they cut a road through the woods, and built a timber roadbed strong and smooth enough for the trucks to travel on. Then they started her and eventually she went. Cables broke, and had to be replaced with stronger ones. Some days she progressed only a few feet. It took months to cover the distance but it was done, and finally the *No. 50* lay broadside to Bakers Bay.

There the salvage crew built an incline of planking down into the water, greased it as the ways are greased at a launching in a shipyard, stretched lines from bow, stern and masts to powerful steam tugs, steadied her with guy ropes, and presently a long pull, a strong pull, a pull all together and the land-locked ship slid down the beach and was afloat once again.

The lightship was then towed to Astoria where she was repaired and eventually returned to her station.

Many similar salvage ventures have been attempted on the ocean shores of the world, many having ended in complete failure. The *No. 50's* land voyage was a notable performance, novel, and successful.

British Ship *Poltalloch*

The 2,250-ton British ship *Poltalloch*, owned by Potter Brothers, of London, was enroute to Puget Sound to load grain for the United Kingdom on November 27, 1900. Off the Washington shore a heavy fog shrouded the coastline and the vessel's position was erroneously charted. She went on the sands at the entrance to Shoalwater Bay opposite North Cove, where the outgoing tide left her high and dry, resting on the sands. The crew dropped the Jacob's ladder over the side and walked ashore.

Hopes of refloating the vessel ran high as her position was not dangerous. Hundreds of spectators were attracted by the spectacle, and the wreck was promptly labeled, "the ship on a voyage to nowhere."

After several months, the *Poltalloch* was removed from the sands, but the interesting incident of the stranding occurred in February, 1902, when the German bark *Professor Koch* was making her way towards the Columbia River. Her helmsman sighted a large square rigger dead ahead. He set his course for the ship unaware that he was inbound for Shoalwater Bay and that the vessel by which he had set his couse was the *Poltalloch,* aground on the sands.

With the crew aloft, shortening sail, the bark edged toward the bar when all at once churning through the swell came the steamer *Fulton* which pulled up alongside the German sailer waving a white flag.

"Where ya heading?" shouted a voice from the wheelhouse of the steamer.

A massive ruddy faced German leaned over the side, and informed the inquirer that he was following the ship dead ahead across the bar.

"Ya damn fool," was the retort, "that there ship's aground, and the tide ain't right for you to cross."

"Is not der Columbia bar?" bellowed the *Koch's* skipper.

"Hell No!" chuckled the steamboater, "You're off Shoalwater."

As a red hue fell over the German captain's face, his ship came slowly about and stood out to sea.

American Steam Schooner *Washington*

One of the most remarkable feats of daring in the history of the north Pacific occurred on November 17, 1911, when Captain C. T. "Buck" Bailey of the tug

Tatoosh gambled with death in shoal infested waters to get a line on the steam schooner *Washington,* fast aground on Peacock Spit.

The *Washington* was heavily laden with lumber when she went on the spit, and her delicate position had shoreside bets running ten to one that she would be a total loss.

For twenty endless hours the steamer was buffeted by nasty seas, while aboard an unsung heroine, Mrs. Mary Fullmer, the only woman among the passengers, kept up the courage of all hands with humor and song.

Certainly under the circumstances it would have been an extremely dangerous task to attempt to rescue the passengers, but Bailey wasn't content with that, for he planned to save all or nothing, and when he accomplished the former, it proved the feat of the decade.

In his own modest words, Captain Bailey explained the deed after the *Washington* had been towed to safety.

"As I approached the *Washington,*" said Bailey, "I could see twelve or fifteen passengers huddled together on the after end of the ship with life-preservers on.

"I asked the captain if he had any steam to use in heaving the hawser aboard. He told me no, that the fires were out. Then I called to the passengers huddled aft and asked them to go forward and help get the hawser aboard. They did so, all of them running over the deckload of lumber and the debris like scared sheep.

"In about ten minutes' time we got the hawser aboard and it was made fast. Finally we started out with the *Washington* in tow. We came slowly through the breakers. I arrived down off the whistling buoy with the *Washington* at 3:45 o'clock. The passengers and crew acted like they were mad when we got started—threw up their hands, gesticulated and yelled at the tops of their voices. I looked over to North Head, and at the lifesaving station, and there must have been a thousand people there watching the rescue."

Later it was revealed that the *Washington* did not have a cent of insurance on her when rescued by the *Tatoosh*.

In writing to George Plummer, manager of the Puget Sound Tow Boat Company, owners of the *Tatoosh*, Bailey said that he did not care if he received a cent of salvage money for saving the *Washington*, but wished that his crew could be rewarded. The tug was valued at $91,000, a considerable gamble on such a venture. Olson & Mahoney of San Francisco, owners of the *Washington* settled with the tug's operators in a case that commanded the attention of many shipping men.

American Schooner *North Bend*

So amazing was the story of the schooner that saved herself, that Robert Ripley once carried the account in his "Believe It Or Not." This vessel was the schooner *North Bend;* she gained her freedom after resting on a sand spit for thirteen months.

While inbound from Adelaide, eighty-nine days out for Astoria, the four master, commanded by Captain Theodore Hansen, attempted to cross the Columbia bar without a pilot. Turning on the ranges at the mouth of the river, the wind suddenly died, and the windjammer stranded off buoy No. 8, near Peacock Spit, at 2:30 a. m., February 5, 1928.

At daybreak the diesel tug *Arrow No. 3,* plowed her way across the bar and made a gallant effort to pull the schooner free. The tug got a hawser on the vessel but while taking up the slack the line parted. On the second attempt the tug got the *North Bend* off the spit and for a moment she was moving into deep water when a terrific sea struck her, breaking the hawser and tossing the schooner back on the spit.

While the salvage attempt was being carried out, the Cape Disappointment, Coast Guardsmen removed the crew of the schooner.

During the ensuing days heavy seas and high winds put the *North Bend* higher on the beach where she remained intact, free from the danger of breaking up. The crew returned and stood by for several days, until all attempts to salvage the vessel were abandoned.

For an entire year the schooner braved the elements remaining virtually undamaged, and the position of the ship's hull aided the sands in playing one of those freak pranks of nature. The winter gales drove in seas that washed the sand away from the vessel and helped form a half mile channel leading into the waters of Bakers Bay. With little aid of the human variety the vessel refloated herself and was edged down the channel to the bay on February 11, 1929, thirteen months after the stranding had occurred.

The Arrow Tug & Barge Company of Astoria, owners of the tug *Arrow No. 3,* purchased the schooner and converted her into a barge after finding her hull in excellent condition.

Except for the dying era of sail, the *North Bend* might have returned to the sea lanes with a new suit of canvas.

Norwegian Motorship *Childar*

Averting the fate that befell the *Laurel,* the Norwegian freighter *Childar* was saved from complete destruction by the uncanny salvage job performed by the Coast Guard cutter *Redwing,* off Peacock Spit, in a southwest gale that ripped along the coast on May 3, 1934.

The night was stormy along the lower reaches of the Columbia River as the motorship *Childar* moved cautiously through the drizzling rain and fog that filtered the river mouth. The *Childar* was down to her marks with a deckload of several million feet of lumber. The pilot called for constant course changes. Soundings were ringing in his ears and the ship's telegraph was jingling every few minutes. A gale was blowing outside and the wind whistled in weird crescendos through the rigging. Without warning a wall of pyramiding water poured against the side of the vessel rolling her wildly and smashing in her number one lifeboat.

That the vessel was working herself into shallow water was indicated by the terrific rolls that picked her up and plunged her into deep troughs. Losing all headway, the ship stood motionless for a brief moment and then was struck by a lunging comber that almost raised her keel completely out of water. The chain gripes which held the deckload snapped like rubber bands and the lumber began to sway wildly as though it were not sure of its freedom. Then with a thundering crash it let go and spread itself all over the decks like kindling. With each breaker the timbers smashed against the foc'sle and then against the superstructure, battering and gouging. The ship labored as the surf poured over the deck while the crew rigged lifelines.

The careening timbers carried all loose gear over the side. Navigation was all but impossible. The howling of the storm was suddenly broken by the rending of steel plates and parting rivets. The *Childar* was aground on the southwest tip of Peacock Spit.

"Hard aport," was the command, but the vessel failed to come off her perch. She was hung up on the spit and an immediate call for help was sent out.

At Astoria the *Redwing* picked up the message at 7:07 a. m. and immediately got underway. Attempts at further contact with the *Childar* proved unavailing, for immediately after sending the distress message her foremast was carried over the side, taking with it the aerial and the antennae.

In a phenomenal run under command of Lieutenant A. W. Davis, the cutter battled her way against the gale until she located the wreck in the murk of the new day. Edging in as close as possible, a hawser was shot over to the stranded freighter. Right down to the leeward the *Redwing* was surrounded by the ship's wreckage. The crew of the *Childar* was too weak to haul the steel hawser aboard which necessitated shooting a lighter twelve- -inch hemp line which the Norwegians proved successful in handling. The line was made fast and the *Redwing* moved cautiously ahead until the slack grew taut. The *Childar* appeared to be sinking and four of five boats had been carried away. The sand and rocks had punctured her plates and a gashing rip at No. 4 hold was evident.

Her smashed bulkheads had stood the onslaught of the sea too long and many of them had given way.

In spite of all this the *Redwing* risked the tow, for to leave the vessel aground in her condition would have meant the lives of the entire crew. At first the freighter refused to move and then two mountainous breakers came roaring in, lifting the vessel and enabling the cutter to get her off and begin the pull. The tow handled awkwardly, as the *Childar's* rudder had been stove, but the job had to go on.

Installing an auxiliary wireless set on the *Childar*, her Nordic skipper informed the cutter's commander that the first and second officers had been washed overboard and drowned and that two seamen were dead and others badly injured. In turn the *Redwing's* master called for assistance from the lifeboats at Cape Disappointment and Point Adams, which promptly came out to remove the injured and dead from the freighter. The boats removed the three most seriously injured by coming up under the *Childar's* counter while the crew lowered their shipmates over the stern in slings. While the rescue was being carried out, one of the lifeboat crew broke four of his ribs, but the task was finally completed and the injured were taken to Astoria while the cutter continued the tow.

Fearing that his ship would founder if the *Redwing* took her back across the bar, the *Childar's* master requested that he be towed to Puget Sound. It was a long haul, but Davis realized the danger of negotiating the bar under such circumstances.

The vessel's bitts to which the towing line was secured, weakened by the terrific pounding, ripped out, but fortunately hung up in the bow chocks. If the line had been lost the *Childar* would have gone back on the spit. Already the cutter had been underway for over an hour and was not yet a safe distance from the shore. Toward afternoon the *Redwing's* course was set for Cape Flattery which commenced one of the toughest towing assignments the Coast Guard has ever been called on to perform.

The *Childar's* No. 4 hold was entirely flooded and No. 5 hold was half full of water. The vessel had a sharp list to port and her decks ran free with water. Her cargo was strewn all over the ship and both masts had been carried into the sea and the funnel knocked from it's fittings.

At 8 a. m. that evening the *Redwing* was off Grays Harbor forty-seven miles from where the tow had begun. The *Childar's* captain expressed fear for the lives of his freezing crew and Davis wired the Grays Harbor motor lifeboat to come out and remove them.

Meanwhile the freighter gave signs of breaking up. The lifeboat came out across the bar and fell in company with the two vessels. Eighteen men were removed from the *Childar*, each by jumping into the sea and being pulled aboard the lifeboat and then transferred to the cutter. Only five men remained on the freighter while the motor lifeboat stood by through the night to remove them should the vessel break up.

The following day the *Redwing* was joined by the cutter *Chelan* and the steam tug *Roosevelt* which convoyed the two vessels into Victoria, B. C., where the task ended after fifty-eight hectic hours.

The *Childar,* owned by Wiel & Amundsen of Halden, Norway, was pumped out and repaired at a cost almost equal to the value of the ship.

STERN WHEELER *STATE OF WASHINGTON*

CHAPTER SEVEN

FIRE, EXPLOSION AND COLLISION

Not all disaster occurs in contrary weather. Nothing is more terrifying to the mariner than his ship engulfed in flames or the tearing of rivets and steel in a collision at sea.

American Sternwheeler *Telephone*

By 1887, Columbia River commerce had shown signs of great progress, and river steamers shuttled to every whistle stop along its banks. The route between Portland and Astoria was highly competitive and only the swiftest and most luxurious steamers vied for the trade.

The biggest money maker on the river was the vessel that combined the greatest speed and luxury, and that honor rightfully fell to the steamer *Telephone*, built at Portland in 1885. Her owners claimed that she was the fastest sternwheeler in the world, and her chronicles upheld her right to that boast. Her glory never faltered until fire gutted her near Astoria on November 20, 1887.

Captain U. B. Scott, master and builder of the *Telephone* was a former Ohio River skipper who took delight in showing his heels to the slower river boats. He had become wealthy by collecting bets from challenging steamboat captains who had tried in vain to outspeed the *Telephone*.

On November 20, the *Telephone* was darting toward Astoria well ahead of schedule when fire broke out amidships throwing pillars of flame and smoke in every direction. Panic broke out among the passengers, and Scott, who was acquainted with the peril of fire, quickly grabbed the wheel and gave it full left rudder and headed directly for the river bank. The steamer scraped over the beach doing nineteen knots. The jolt sent the passengers sprawling.

The crew attempted to restore order to protect the 140 passengers from being trampled to death, but the decks were so hot that the tourists stampeded to the railings and scrambled over the guards in droves. One by one they dropped to the mud on the beach and struggled to reach higher land.

Flames engulfed the bridge, and Captain Scott was forced to jump through the pilot house window after discovering that the ladder had burned away. By the time he had reached safety, Astoria's horse-drawn fire wagons were winging their way over the washboard road leading down to the river bank. Spectators, startled by the blaze, came from miles around to see the steamer burn.

Oblivious to the blazing inferno, an inebriate had remained aboard groping his way about until he was overcome by the fumes. The burned ashes of his body

were found among the remains of the ship. Fortune-
ately he proved to be the only casualty, though several
others suffered from burns and injuries.

The housing of the steamer burned like tinder while
hoses played streams of water on her from every angle.
Only through the ceaseless work of the firemen was the
vessel's hull saved, but nothing more.

The charred remains lay abandoned for several
months, but later from them was born a new *Telephone*, more lavish than her forerunner, but unable
to break the speed record of the original boat which
had to her credit a spectacular run between Portland
and Astoria of four hours, thirty-four and one-half
minutes.

American Schooner *Challenger*

Near South Bend, the schooner *Challenger* reposed
on the river bottom in fourteen feet of water where
she was sunk November 7, 1904, to quell a blaze that
had licked at her for eleven days.

The story of the hardship endured by the crew of
the *Challenger* is best related by her master, Captain
H. Nelson.

"I left Fort Blakely, October 24, 1904, for San Francisco and was becalmed four days in the Straits. After
passing Cape Flattery we had a northeast wind for
twelve hours, when the wind suddenly changed to the
southeast and blew up a hurricane. The ship labored
heavily.

"On October 29, two seamen were washed overboard, but although the sea was high they were picked
up. The gale kept on increasing till November 4, when
I discovered smoke issuing from the cabin. I discovered
the ship was on fire.

"We crowded on all sail to make port and lost much
canvas. At noon on November 4, we were off Tillamook Bay, but could not get in because of mountain-

ous seas. We then steered for the Columbia River. By this time no man could stand at the wheel because of the smoke and fumes from the lime cargo. We signalled to the Columbia River tug, but the bar was too rough for one to come out. I hailed the lightship but could get no help and then made for Willapa Harbor.

"The tug *Astoria* was inside but was afraid to cross till I hoisted distress signals, when Captain Chris Olsen of the tug came out and took me in tow. In crossing the bar the sea washed over the tug and Captain Olsen was knocked down and badly hurt I later found out. I was towed to South Bend, and two hours later flames broke through the cabin and the schooner had to be scuttled."

Captain Nelson and his crew were all treated for burns, congested lungs and internal injuries at the town hospital. They had been without water for six days after the fresh water tanks had become flooded with sea water.

What little equipment remained aboard the *Challenger* was salvaged, but unfortunately the vessel's owners, the Pacific Stevedoring and Ballasting Company, of San Francisco, carried no insurance on the schooner. She was loaded with 3800 barrels of Roche Harbor lime and 150,000 feet of lumber which constantly fed the flames.

When the government dredge was working on the Willapa River in April, 1934, it scooped up parts of the old schooner from the river bottom where it had reposed undisturbed for thirty years.

Collision of the *Welsh Prince* and *Iowan*

It was 11:10 p. m., May 28, 1922, and the lower Columbia was blanketed by a persistent fog which reached in from the Pacific. Inside the Columbia entrance off Altoona Head, two large freighters were cautiously feeling their way. One was the British steamer *Welsh Prince* and the other the American freighter *Iowan.*

The night was still but for foghorns issuing mournful cries. Suddenly the stillness was broken by the sickening crash of cold steel tearing and grinding. The *Iowan,* commanded by Captain L. LaVerge, had rammed her prow into the side of the *Welsh Prince* and the night air was filled with human cries of agony.

It was so foggy that neither ship was visible to the other until an orange flame suddenly loomed up from the British vessel.

"We're afire!" came a voice from out of the haze.

Without hesitation the hoses on both ships were attached and trained on the location of the flames. Bit by bit the blaze was extinguished and then all hands were assembled to survey the extent of the damage. The *Iowan* had nearly severed the *Welsh Prince* forward, and had badly crumpled her own bow in the procedure. Aboard the *Welsh Prince* the situation was far more serious for seven seamen had been crushed to death in the foc'sle, and the vessel was settling fast.

Receiving the distress calls, the tug *Oneonta* set out from Astoria and felt her way through the fog till she reached the scene of the collision. Five bodies were removed from the water-filled forecastle, but the remaining two were not found until the extreme tide.

The vessels were separated and the *Iowan* was taken up river to Portland for badly needed repairs.

When the fog lifted the *Welsh Prince* was at the bottom of the river with only her upper works above water.

After several attempts to raise her had failed, Frank Waterhouse & Company, agents for the sunken ship, notified her owners, the Furness Prince Line, of London, that she must be considered a total loss. The wreck became a hazard to navigation and the only way to remove it from the river bottom was through the use of high potency dynamite.

M. Barde & Sons were employed by the government to remove the wreck, but being unable to accomplish the task, employed a dynamiter to finish the job. Accordingly, ten tons of super-power gelatin dynamite were ordered from the Du Pont plant near Olympia. The deck of the *Welsh Prince* was blown off to remove the cargo of steel and later the hull was blasted to pieces in a thundering explosion that was felt for miles around the mouth of the river. When the geyser of water had cleared away the hazard to navigation was non-existent.

EARLY PILOT SCHOONER

CHAPTER EIGHT

MYSTERY SHIPS

Nothing so arouses man's imagination as the tale of a ship that sails out to sea and disappears with all hands. Theory and fantasy are often derived from man's imagination as a substitute for what he cannot explain. From these yarns have come tales of the "Flying Dutchman," so widespread that each maritime nation has its own story of those specter ships that sail the lonely seas.

American Bark *Vandalia*

She was sighted by Captain Phillips of the brig *Grecian* on January 9, 1853. He stated that she appeared to be laboring, but was in no need of assistance. That was all that was heard of the *Vandalia* till a week later when she was carried ashore bottom up near McKenzie Head.

Four bodies floated ashore near the wreck, one of which was identified as Captain E. N. Beard, master of the *Vandalia*. His remains drifted into a rocky indentation which since that day has been known as Beard's Hollow.

Among the three other bodies was that of a fourteen-year-old boy.

The cause of the disaster was never known but the supposition was that the vessel had missed stays while beating in towards the bar and had drifted into the breakers. She probably fouled her bottom, filled and capsized, which may or may not fill the missing link to the tragic loss, which caused the death of twelve seafarers.

American Schooner *Sunshine*

The *Sunshine* was constructed at Marshfield, Oregon, and completed in September, 1875, by Holden & Company for E. B. Deane and Associates, at a cost of $32,000. She was a three-masted schooner of 326 tons and was hailed as a shipbuilding triumph on Coos Bay.

The vessel was placed in command of Captain George Bennett, who shared an interest in the ownership of the schooner. On her maiden voyage from Coos Bay she arrived at San Francisco on October 8, 1875, to discharge a cargo of lumber. For the return passage the *Sunshine* carried machinery and general cargo. In addition, several passengers were booked and her complement numbered twenty-five in all.

Captain Bennett had an excellent record as a mariner and carried two officers of equal repute: John Thompson and Joseph Johnson.

On the return leg of her maiden voyage, the *Sunshine* passed through the Golden Gate on November 3, and was not seen again till fifteen days later when sighted bottom up off Cape Disappointment. On November 22 the derelict washed ashore on the peninsula, but no clue to the disappearence of her company was found among the wreckage.

The experts claimed that, owing to the newness of the schooner, she was stiff and perhaps difficult to operate, but her builders countered with the fact that she had been built of seasoned timbers. Both held to the hope that some of her complement might be picked up at sea to answer the query but the sea refused to give up its dead.

As is the case with all mysteries of the sea, fantasy is bound to creep in and add its tantalizing flavor to the little known facts. It is recorded that the *Sunshine's* cargo was valued at $18,000, and in addition she carried more than $10,000 in gold coin which was being sent to her builders at Coos Bay from interests in San Francisco, who shared a part ownership in the vessel.

There were some who claimed that the schooner was purposely destroyed by conniving passengers who escaped in a boat with the keg of gold after first killing the others.

Then there was another story hinting that the vessel had previously gone aground fifteen miles north of Coos Bay and that a barrel of coin was buried in the sands by an officer. Later the schooner was said to have been carried back to sea and left at the mercy of the winds, later capsizing and going ashore again on the peninsula.

The latter tale is actually known to have started people digging in the sands north of Coos Bay in search of the gold—which incidentally has yet to be found.

Not the slightest clue to the fate of the twenty-five souls aboard the schooner has ever been forthcoming.

Pilot Schooner *J. C. Cousins*

The mighty Pacific holds many unsolved mysteries and tales of intrigue, but none is more baffling than the drama that was enacted in the waters of the Pacific's Graveyard within view of the shore on October 7, 1883. It involved the wreck of a pilot schooner and the disappearence of her crew.

The pilot schooner was a craft of excellent lines, with cabins of the finest hardwoods and elaborate fittings. She was a two-masted vessel and bore the name, *J. C. Cousins.* Her beauty resulted from her originally having been built to the orders of a wealthy Californian as his private schooner-yacht. Several months later he was forced to sell her. The vessel was purchased at San Francisco in 1881, and brought to the Columbia River in March of the same year to run in opposition to Captain Flavel's monopoly in bar piloting. The schooner was operated as a pilot boat by the State of Oregon for two years prior to her mysterious loss.

When the *J. C. Cousins* first arrived on the Columbia, she was commanded by Captain George Woods, and was jointly operated by Captain Charles Richardson, H. A. Matthews, Thomas Powers and Henry Olsen, all of Astoria.

The schooner loaded supplies at Astoria on October 6, 1883, and as usual had stood out to sea to meet incoming vessels. Aboard were four men in charge of the boatkeeper whose name is remembered only as Zeiber.

It was near noon when the schooner passed Fort Stevens. Later in the afternoon she was sighted at anchor off Clatsop Spit. On the same day the tug *Mary Taylor* sighted the *Cousins* sail out through the breakers near Clatsop Spit and then at dusk reverse her course and stand in for the bar. She continued those strange antics until she was lost in the darkness.

At daybreak other ships reported sighting the pilot vessel sometimes standing in towards shore and then again tacking offshore and moving out to sea. At 1 p. m. on October 7, the *Cousins* was reported nearly three miles at sea when suddenly the wind changed and she came about and headed for Clatsop Spit. About 2:15 p.m. she reached the surf but this time failed to come about and instead came in through the breakers and was swept hard on the beach.

Several persons who had been following the strange course of the pilot schooner hastened to the scene but were unable to get near the wreck until low tide.

Not a living soul nor a dead one was found aboard the schooner. A further search revealed that the boat was missing as was the logbook and papers. Everything else appeared to be in proper order.

A few days later the seas broke up the vessel, leaving no further clue to the disappearance of the crew.

When the ensuing weeks failed to divulge any word of the missing seamen, the maritime sleuths and yarn spinners settled down to some deep thinking. One theory was advanced that gained considerable acceptance.

It was claimed that Zeiber had been engaged to wreck the *Cousins*, kill his shipmates and then disappear, thus destroying competition against the Flavel monopoly. This story was backed by mariners from Astoria who in later years were said to have actually seen Zeiber in Oriental ports.

Such a scheme seemed highly improbable, however, as the operators of the *Cousins* immediately following her loss chartered the centerboard sloop *City of Napa* to continue the opposition until the state could build the pilot schooner *Governor Moody*.

Other theories of sea monsters and mutiny were advanced. One demented old beachcomber told how a great ghost ship had borne down on the *Cousins* and frightened the crew so badly that they took to the boat for fear of being rammed. He claimed that he had once seen this same ghost ship coming across the bar.

When the waterfront folk of Astoria would laugh at the old timer, a sinister look would come over his face and he would shake his bony finger at them.

"It is real, I tell ye," he would frown. "A ship of the dead that sails the sea, with a ghostly crew. In the tempest she appears, and before the gale or agin the gale. She sails without a rag of canvas and without a helmsman at the wheel," he would sputter as he hobbled down the river bank cursing his unappreciative audience.

Perhaps the only logical solution given was that the schooner struck on the bar while outbound, which frightened the crew who in turn took the boat. The heavy swell probably swamped the craft, throwing the men into the water and drowning them.

How long the schooner sailed without a crew was never established and the case has remained unsolved to this day.

American Steamship *Drexel Victory*

An air of mystery still hangs about the maritime courts concerning the loss of the steamship *Drexel Victory*.

At 5 p. m., January 19, 1947, the freighter, out bound from Portland for Yokohama with 5000 tons of grain and general cargo, either structually collapsed, struck Peacock Spit, or rammed the remains of a sunken wreck, while in transit across the bar.

The vessel, carrying forty-nine officers and men, was in charge of bar pilot E. P. Gillette, and her master was Captain Canute Rommerdahl.

While crossing the bar, the *Drexel Victory* suddenly

cracked between holds No. 4 and 5. Water gushed through the break and her plates bulged from her frames like water blisters—seepage was everywhere. The crew were at the pumps but were unable to control the influx of sea water.

The situation became hopeless, and Rommerdahl had to give the order to abandon ship.

The Coast Guard motor lifeboat *Triumph,* the pilot ship *Columbia,* the cutter *Onondaga* and the liberty freighter *Joseph Gale* all stood by. In spite of the blackness of the night the crew was taken off without mishap.

The sinking freighter drifted over the bar and the cutter *Onondaga* took out in pursuit in an attempt to get a line on her and beach her in shallow water. Darkness closed in all around and at 1:30 a. m. the freighter plunged to the bottom in deep water one-quarter mile due west of buoy No. 6, after drinking up gallons of ocean water.

The survivors were landed at Astoria.

Following the hearing over the loss, the Oregon State Board of River Pilot Examiners exonerated Captain Gillette of any responsibility in the sinking of the vessel. The board held that Gillette while piloting the ship over the bar, had discharged all his duties in a competent manner.

Gillette in turn suggested that structural failure might have caused the trouble, but expressed doubt that the vessel had actually grounded.

"When she struck," stated Gillette, "she was in fifty-nine to sixty-one feet of water—that is if she did strike."

According to further reports at the hearing it was brought out that the *Drexel Victory* was drawing twenty-nine to thirty feet of water when her hull cracked. She was in the proper ship channel and had taken some heavy swells though the bar was not rough.

Following the incident, Colonel O. E. Walsh, of the Corps of Engineers, ordered a further survey of the spot where the freighter was said to have struck, but the investigation revealed that the channel was deep and unobstructed as the charts indicated.

The *Drexel Victory* was operated by Oliver Olson & Company and was owned by the U. S. Maritime Commission. She was a Victory type vessel of 7,607 gross tons and was built at Richmond, California, in 1945.

BARK *HARVEST HOME*

CHAPTER NINE

AGROUND IN THE FOG

Fog—the persistant enemy of the mariner; a ghostly vapor that creeps in silently and obscures the headlands and closes the boundaries of the world.

Before the advent of radio and radar now so vital to mariners, the Pacific's Graveyard was a shore of ill-repute. Fog spread in from the sea blotting out flashing lights while storms pressing shoreward muzzled the most persistant foghorns, none too plentiful fifty years ago. Even in our present age ships still fall victim to fog.

110

American Bark *Harvest Home*

If it is possible for a shipwreck to be a happy affair, perhaps the loss of the bark *Harvest Home* would fall under this classification. The date was January 18, 1882, and the bark was beating up the coast under a pleasant breeze in a calm sea shrouded by a white sheet of fog. Her destination was Port Townsend and she rode low in the water with a full load of general cargo.

Under the command of Captain A. Matson, the bark was skirting along in a northwesterly course in the early morning hours while most of the crew were asleep. Only the sea water caressing the hull of the vessel broke the silence of the nearing dawn. Then came another sound, a sound quite divorced from those of the sea. The helmsman cupped his hand to his ear and then pinched himself—had he heard a rooster crowing or was he dreaming?

Suddenly the vessel began to pitch and roll as though it had been struck by a tidal wave. The crew was tossed from the bunks and loose gear rolled over the deck. In a matter of minutes the ship was deposited on the sands and suddenly became motionless.

Captain Matson stormed up on deck and leaped up on the poop, but before he could get his mouth open, the helmsman informed him that the vessel was aground.

"Aground you say, Mister, why we're six miles to sea, I set the course myself," bellowed the Old Man.

Fog was all about the stranded ship, but there was little doubt about her being aground, and before the flood tide had decided to go back to sea again the *Harvest Home* was bogged down in the sand up around the driftwood area.

Several hours later the bewildered skipper discovered that he had been navigating with a defective chronometer which was responsible for the stranding.

When the fog lifted around noon, the helmsman sighted a big barn a few hundred feet from the beach, and it was then that he knew that the rooster he had heard crowing had not been a figment of his imagination. The wreck was lying eight miles north of Cape Disappointment, on the sandy beach of the peninsula.

Later the crew walked ashore and the wreck remained stationary while the tides swished around her, more firmly entrenching her in the sands. The cargo was salvaged but the bark was left to die a slow death.

In the months that followed tourists paused at the wreck to have their pictures taken under the summer sun or to picnic on her rotting timbers. Some of the shipwrecked sailors found themselves pretty peninsula belles and tied the legal knot of matrimony.

Meanwhile Preston & McKinnon of San Francisco, owners of the *Harvest Home,* collected $14,000, the amount for which the vessel was insured.

Pilot Schooner *Governor Moody*

It will be recalled that the loss of the pilot schooner *J. C. Cousins* prompted the chartering of the sloop *City of Napa* until the State of Oregon had completed the building of the pilot schooner *Governor Moody* at Astoria in 1885. The new sixty-four-ton vessel operated until November 20, 1890, when she was cast ashore on the rocks off North Head.

In command of Captain Peter Cordiner, the *Moody* moved silently through the fog-filtered waters off the river entrance. It was early morning and daybreak was awaited to meet an inbound vessel seeking pilotage.

At 4 a. m. the schooner was tossed about violently and the crew rallied forward and discovered the craft was trapped in dangerous waters frequented with swirling eddies. The sails were put aback but the wind refused to fill them and the currents swept the vessel on the rocks, badly fouling her bottom.

The men sprang to the shrouds as the seas came over the weather rail and covered the decks. Her bow dropped and reappeared with gallons of green water rolling aft. The foremast was knocked from its fittings and plumeted into the water wedging itself against a rock jutting from the sea a short distance from the schooner. Sloshing around in knee-deep water the frightened seamen straddled the fallen mast and inched their bodies across the rock to gain temporary refuge from the rampaging surf.

When the fog cleared, the wreck was sighted by the lighthouse keepers on Cape Disappointment, who in turn passed the word to the Fort Canby lifesaving crew. The surf boat put out from the station and picked up the shivering sailors from the rock and then took the fallen mast in tow. The pilot schooner swamped within the day and became a total loss.

The schooner *San Jose* was later purchased at San Francisco by Pilot Commissioner P. W. Weeks to fill the vacancy left by the *Governor Moody*.

British Bark *Cairnsmore*

When salt water mixes with 7500 barrels of cement in a ship's hold, that vessel will become preserved in the sands of time.

The British bark *Cairnsmore*, Captain B. Gibbs, master, was inbound for Portland from London, but was hampered by a veil of fog which had made navigation difficult. Though Gibbs knew he was in the vicinity of the Columbia River entrance, he was unable to gain his bearings until after breakers were sighted at 10:30 a. m. on September 26, 1883. The vessel was down to her marks with a heavy load of cement and machinery, and she labored in the surf defying all efforts to put her head into the wind.

"Aloft and get 'em in!" yelled the bucko mate. The crew scurried up the rigging and strung themselves along the yardarms, standing in the swaying footropes. With bleeding fingers, clutching and clawing at the stubborn acres of canvas, they struggled to haul them in and wrap the gaskets around them.

But it was too late; the vessel struck the sands with a thud. Signal flares soared into the air but were swallowed by the fog.

For fifteen hours the sailors worked to free the ship and finally were forced to man the boats and row out to sea instead of risking their lives in the heavy surf. The boats bobbed in an ocean that seemed to set them apart from the rest of the world.

Suddenly from out of the fog came the sound of a deep-throated whistle which gradually grew louder.

SAILING SHIP *GLENMORAG*

Oars were shipped and all eyes peered into the murk. Parting the strands of fog appeared the bow of a steamer knifing her way through the sea. Less than a hundred yards away, the whistle blasted again, and the men stood up in the boats and yelled at the tops of their voices.

Fortunately their cries were heard by the watch on the bridge wing; the engine room bell clanged and the ship's forward motion decreased as it veered off to starboard. As the lifeboats rowed toward the steamer the crew made out the name *Queen of the Pacific* scrolled on her bows; the same ship that had been ashore on Clatsop Spit three weeks earlier.

The shipwrecked seamen were taken aboard, and the liner crept on towards the bar and faded into the fog.

The following day a salvage crew went to the scene of the wreck to investigate possibilities of saving the ship and her cargo. They soon discovered that water had leaked into the hull and that the cement was seeping through the barrel staves. The ship lay in an exposed position and the situation grew more hopeless as day by day the cement escaped from the barrels and hardened. Several months later the hull was consumed by the sands and sealed in a casket of cement.

The *Cairnsmore,* a 1,200-ton bark, was valued at $48,000 and her cargo was insured for $18,000.

British Ship *Glenmorag*

The ship *Glenmorag,* of Glascow, departed New York August 16, 1895, and arrived at Melbourne after a lengthy run of 103 days. In the South Atlantic she was trapped in an icefield frequented by more than a hundred bergs, which nearly spelled her doom. She set sail for Astoria in ballast, arriving off the mouth of the Columbia on March 18, 1896. The following day the vessel was fog-bound and becalmed except for the prevailing northerly drift. At 3:30 p. m. the lookout sighted breakers and the big square rigger went on the beach seven miles north of Ilwaco.

The thick fog obscured the ship's grounding from the shore.

Two hours later a knock was heard at the door of a resident on the peninsula. A man answered and was met by a ragged seaman who requested help for his shipmates on the wrecked ship.

The *Glenmorag* had struck at high tide broadside to, and two boats were lowered and cleared away. The mate in charge of one boat attempted to pull out to sea but the surf drove him toward shore forcing the craft to weather the breakers. The other boat in rounding the stern of the *Glenmorag* was caught by a tremendous sea and dashed up under the counter killing two seamen and injuring the others. The boat was badly damaged but was kept afloat by the air-tight tanks, and was eventually carried up on the beach.

Captain Archibald Currie, master of the *Glenmorag*, later lowered another boat and with the remainder of the crew reached the shore in safety.

In all, twenty-seven persons were aboard the vessel at the time of the wreck. The dead were John Reedy and James Adams.

Among the injured was a seaman named William Begg. When he reached the shore a young lady from Oysterville removed his wet shoes and gave him warm blankets. Several months later he married her and the couple settled down on the peninsula. They still live there today (1950) in a stately old dwelling that was built by Begg.

Visiting their home is like stepping into the past, for such items as the dinner bell and kitchenware salvaged from the galley of the *Glenmorag* are still in use.

Captain Currie later conferred with the British Consul concerning the wreck and the possibilities of salvage. The *Glenmorag* had received only minor damage in the mishap and several attempts were later made to refloat her. In December the ship was moved forty feet and local authorities reported that she would soon be afloat. On the day of the scheduled refloating the tide was full, the cables and winches in place and tugs were standing by. The *Glenmorag* was pulled to freedom momentarily, but was struck by a series of wicked breakers which carried her back on the beach, this time for good.

The ship was then dismantled by Kern & Kern of Portland, and everything of value was stripped from her. The remains were abandoned and eventually devoured by the sands. About sixty feet of her steel hull were uncovered by the shifting sands in the winter of 1948, but were covered again within the month. The *Glenmorag's* memory is kept green, however, by the existence of her figurehead representing a stately goddess, now in possession of William Begg.

The loss of so many fine ships on the peninsula in the eighties and nineties led to speculation that unscrupulous shipowners were conniving with the ship masters to run their commands ashore and collect the insurance costs.

German Bark *Potrimpos*

A strong wind and heavy sea prevailed as the Ilwaco lifesaving crew trudged along the beach to reach the wreck of the German bark *Potrimpos* on December 19, 1896. A large white horse was pulling the cart that carried the surf boat, but in the severe storm the animal became frightened and balked, refusing to pull the load any farther. Despite the whip, the horse would not go on. In desperation the lifesaving crew struggled with the cart and pulled it up to the track of the pioneer Ilwaco-Nahcotta Railroad which ran the length of the peninsula. They awaited the arrival of the engine and when she came they halted it and loaded the equipment on a flatcar and continued to the scene of the wreck—minus the horse.

The lifesaving crew found that six seamen had already made the beach in a boat, but that their services were urgently needed in rescuing twelve others. The surf boat put out from the beach and succeeded in bringing the remainder of the shipwrecked sailors ashore.

When the tide had receded, the steel bark was fully a hundred yards from the surf. Salvage work was immediately commenced and after several months of unsuccessful attempts to get her off the sands, the big chance came, but ended in near disaster. The Spreckles tug *Relief* was standing by and the hawsers and donkey engines were placed in strategic places for easing the hull into the surf. With the salvage crew aboard, the vessel was inched over the sands at the given hour, but the ballast had been removed from her hull and she floated high. When they got her into the breakers she suddenly careened over on her beam ends and the lives of the salvage crew were in grave peril.

The *Potrimpos'* bell was washed up on the beach at the feet of young Gilbert Tinker, who had played hookey from school to watch the salvage operations. Startled by the sudden turn of events, he picked up the bell and ran into town to get aid for the stranded salvage crew. Later the trapped salvagers were brought ashore and treated for their injuries.

Tinker still lives near Long Beach (1950) and fondly recalls how he found the *Potrimpos'* bell on that fateful day in the spring of 1897. He remembers the straining donkey engines, the taut hawsers and the smoking tug a quarter of a mile offshore. Then there came that tragic moment when the vessel flipped over on her side.

At a hearing concerning the stranding of the *Potrim-pos,* Captain Hellwegge, her master stated: "My ship the *Potrimpos,* was out of Hamburg and had made a call at Manzanillo to discharge. Booking no cargo there we were ordered to sail for the Columbia River in ballast to pick up a cargo of grain at Portland. When near the river, I was aware of the proximity of land, and was sure I was off the mouth of the Columbia. I was constantly on the lookout for the pilot boat or a tug, but the vessel drifted northward with the wind and current, becoming helpless before we could bring her back to sea."

American Schooner *Solano*

A vessel that might well be referred to as the ghost ship of the peninsula, is the four-masted schooner *Solano* which grounded four miles north of Ocean Park, February 5, 1907. For several years her hull arose and disappeared in the sands, and then in 1923, it vanished for nearly ten years and had almost been forgotten

SCHOONER *SOLANO*

when the shifting sands uncovered it once again. It has remained visible since the early thirties, becoming a landmark on the beach. Her hatches are banked with sand where shellfish move around in deep pools formed by high tides. Her back is broken and only stumps stand where once tall masts shot skyward. Her timbers have been bleached almost white by the salt water and wind and sand.

In the summer of 1947 vacationers built a bonfire inside the old craft and neglecting to smother it on their departure the sparks ignited the timbers, and the local fire fighters were summoned to extinguish the blaze.

Fog, storm, surf and fire have failed to put an end to the old wreck and she languishes on amid her strange surroundings in a sea of sand.

The most common question of the visitor to the peninsula is, "How did she get there?"

It was early morning in the winter of 1907, when the North Beach lifesaving crew received word that a schooner had gone aground. The lookout in the station tower sighted distress signals several miles down the beach rising above the low hanging fog. Within a few moments the beach equipment and the men in their storm gear were plodding their way toward the scene of the flares. The surf was exceptionally calm for a winter day and they encountered little difficulty in getting the shipwrecked seamen ashore.

At low water the schooner was found to be undamaged and immediately plans were undertaken to re-float her.

Ten months later the scene was set. A large salvage crew under the direction of W. H. Wood of the Hart-Wood Lumber Company had worked ceaselessly to prepare the vessel for re-launching and on the high tide of December, 1908, the task was successfully accomplished with the aid of the flood tide.

Wood had made arrangements with the owners of the tug *Daring*, of Astoria, to be there at the designated time of the schooner's refloating so that she could be towed safely to port. All had gone according to schedule except that the tug failed to make an appearance. Anxiously, Wood scanned the horizon but the tug was nowhere in sight. The *Solano* wallowed in the surf, bucking a strong south wind which created an angry surf. Hour by hour the breakers mounted and finally she was driven back on the beach with tremendous force.

Bewildered, Wood watched his efforts fade before his very eyes. Further attempts to save the *Solano* were abandoned.

At the subsequent litigation, Wood was awarded half of the appraised value of the schooner, less half the tug-boat rate that had been agreed on.

When the schooner first went aground, she was enroute to Grays Harbor from San Francisco. As she lay on the beach a constant watch was kept over her to prevent looting, and it was not an uncommon sight to see a large washing hanging from the rigging each Monday. Strange indeed for a landlocked vessel.

Gazing at her gnarled bones today one can hardly believe that she was once a graceful windship which had to her credit in 1902 a record passage from Shanghai to Port Townsend in the remarkable time of twenty-four days.

Canadian Freighter *Canadian Exporter*

It was just another case of fog that caused the *Canadian Exporter* to go aground at the entrance to Willapa Harbor, August 1, 1921. She was bound for Portland from Vancouver, B. C., to complete loading lumber for the Orient, when she drove up on the sands and defied all efforts to be backed off. When the fog lifted, the tug *Wallula* went to the aid of the steamer but

failed to get her off the shoal. The tug returned later
in the day in company with the salvage steamer *Algerine,* and after removing the crew of the freighter, both
vessels got lines on the ship and put on a great show
of power which failed to produce results.

On the following morning it was discovered that
the *Canadian Exporter* was working on the sands and
showed signs of breaking up. The salvage crew of the
Algerine boarded her and began to remove the loose
deck equipment.   Satisfied that refloating the wreck
was a virtual impossibility, the *Algerine's* party made
preparations for sailing home within the day, but their
plans were interrupted when suddenly the whistle on
the freighter began to blast. Not a soul was aboard her
and the ghostly sounds chilled the observers, as they
stood on the deck of the salvage steamer, their mouths
wide open.

T. W. Allen, superintendent of the salvage operations, immediately ordered a boat over the side to investigate. As the craft drew closer, Allen found that the
freighter was breaking up before his eyes. A large crack

STEAMSHIP *CANADIAN EXPORTER*

aft the bridge widened as it traveled down to the water-
line. As the swells struck against the ship's hull the
wave action on the sagging bow would tighten the
whistle cord, continuing the blast until the cord grew
limp.

Allen was hopeful of boarding the ship again to use
the remaining steam to salvage cargo, but considered
the ship's condition too dangerous to risk the lives of
his crew.

At 7:30 a. m. the *Canadian Exporter* sounded her
own death knell with one final blast of her whistle
followed by the parting of rivets and the rending of
steel. A few minutes later the ship broke in two. With
no further hesitation the salvage steamer sailed out
over the horizon.

The story might have ended here, but for two ad-
venturous gentlemen from Vancouver, B. C., who purchased rights to the wreck from the underwriters for
$2,000. Their names were H. R. McMillan and Percy
Sills.

With each passing day the position of the wreck
grew more dangerous, but the two Canadians gathered
equipment to salvage the lumber and machinery and
made arrangements with Hugh Delanty, prominent
Grays Harbor stevedoring executive, to supply fifteen
of his best longshoremen.

The purchase of the wreck caused considerable
comment up and down the coast and wagers were
placed as to whether or not the salvaging would prove
successful.

With a string of barges and other conveyances, the
work got under way on September 2, 1921. Only the
steering engine was salvaged from the after section of
the wreck, well imbedded in the sands. From the forward section, refrigeration equipment, deck gear and
a quantity of lumber stowed in the holds was salvaged through tenacious efforts.

Lighters were constantly standing by, and a launch brought the workmen to and from the wreck. When the weather was bad the job could not be carried on for the Coast Guard placed tight restrictions on the operation, fearing loss of life.

Near the end of October the wreck had to be abandoned.

When McMillan and Sills added up the accounts, they discovered that they had spent $20,000 in wages and equipment. They sold the lumber and machinery for $17,500, and were left with a deficite of $4,500 including the rights to the wreck. Financially the venture had failed, but the partners agreed that the job was one of the most interesting they had ever undertaken.

The only money makers on the loss of the vessel were the lawyers, there being a protracted litigation over the insurance on the vexed question of deviation.

American Steamship *Admiral Benson*

What was first reported on February 15, 1930 as a minor stranding turned out to be a major steamship disaster.

With thirty-nine passengers, sixty-five crew members and a cargo of citrus fruits and general freight, the liner *Admiral Benson,* of the Pacific Steamship Company, stranded on the sands at Buoy No. 6, near Peacock Spit. It was 6:45 p. m., and the vessel was inbound for Portland when she shoved her nose on the spit in the foggy channel entrance. The stranding appeared so minor that Captain C. C. Graham did not send out an urgent appeal for help, but asked assistance only.

The Coast Guard cutter *Redwing* was ordered out to stand by the *Benson,* but her boilers were cold and she was unable to clear from Astoria until several hours later. The freighter *Nevada* also received the call for assistance and stood by the liner while the Coast Guard lifeboats from Point Adams and Cape Disappointment handled the evacuation of passengers. Many of the tourists were compelled to slide down wet ropes to the rescue craft.

By noon on February 17, most of the passengers had been removed and all efforts were directed towards saving the crew who had remained with the ship hoping to refloat her. The situation appeared less hopeful as a high wind approached and kicked up a nasty surf. By 9:06 a. m. the following morning the five remaining passengers were taken off, followed by the steward's staff and the orchestra.

The wreck was located 400 yards west of the north jetty directly in view of the remains of the *Laurel,* which served as a grim reminder to those still aboard the liner.

The following day, Captain Graham watched the last of the crew go ashore by breeches buoy, and he alone remained aboard the vessel. The holds had been pumped full of water to keep the ship from pounding, but when a forty-mile gale arose, the *Benson* was given a salt bath by mountainous breakers. On the morning of February 20, the riveting began to pull loose and the ship showed signs of breaking up. The decks cracked, the engine room was flooded and the surplus water saturated the cargo in the holds.

On February 21, the redoubtable captain was still aboard, his spirits warmed by the friendly bonfire that was kept burning night and day at Cape Disappointment. It wasn't until four days later that Graham abandoned his vigil, and signalled the Coast Guard for assistance.

A line had been made fast between the wreck and the shore and the ship's master began an arduous journey through the air on a lifesaving conveyance.

The passengers and crew had been landed at Astoria and each had a version of the disaster. Several agreed that the wreck of the *Laurel* had been mistaken for a range buoy, which may have misled the liner to the spit in the fog.

KLIPSAN LIFESAVING STATION

CHAPTER TEN

CONQUERING THE BAR

One of the most difficult ocean bar problems ever attacked by engineers is that of maintaining a channel at the entrance to the Columbia River. Its scope and the difficulties in securing accurate data for engineering computations were widely known. When it is considered that the actual bar area, when improvement work first began, was approximately six miles by six miles the task undertaken is readily appreciated. Then a study of the violence of the storm forces, the tremendous volume of fresh water discharge, and the strength and variations of littoral currents, reveal what the engineer had to cope with when he undertook to confine and control the river discharge and tidal flow.

The aids to navigation along the shores of the Pacific's Graveyard fall into several categories. The first visual aids came with the erection of lookout stations and lighthouses; then the surfboat stations and bar surveys and finally the building of the jetties. It has been a long and arduous task to assure the safety factors that exist in the area today.

The first official survey of the bar conditions was made by Sir Edward Belcher, in the H. M. S. *Sulphur* on his visit to the river in 1839. His findings showed some remarkable changes from the charts of 1792. The northern channel up to Cape Disappointment was then the only known satisfactory entrance. The expedition in 1841 also found but one channel and that was little changed. The next advance in Columbia River bar hydrography was the discovery of the south channel in January, 1850, by Captain White, who found not less than four fathoms on the bar. In 1851, the U. S. Coast Survey under Lieutenant W. P. McArthur completed a preliminary survey of the outer entrance and showed that the north channel had very much altered and was unsafe except for small vessels.

In 1883, the entrance to the Columbia River was five miles wide between the nearest parts of Cape Disappointment and Point Adams, but the passage was greatly obstructed by shifting shoals, which extended in a curve between the entrance points. The north channel had shoaled to a depth of seventeen feet. Sailing vessels could not beat into the south channel against the summer winds blowing from the northwest, but almost invariably could make the outward passage under similar conditions. Heavily laden vessels used the north channel.

At that early date it was recorded that once a mail steamer tried for sixty hours to find the smallest show of an opening to get across the bar when heavy weather broke from the Cape to Point Adams. Sailing vessels have waited as long as six weeks offshore for safe bar transit conditions.

Before the turn of the century, the lifesaving crews played a major role along these stretches. During the summer months fair ladies flocked to the seashore to watch these he-men stage daring sham rescues; but when the storms of winter returned the scene became stark reality.

The initial lifesaving station at the mouth of the Columbia was established at Fort Canby in 1878, although a lookout had been maintained at Cape Disappointment since the building of the light tower in 1856. When wrecks along the North Beach Peninsula increased in number, the Ilwaco Lifesaving Station was erected at Klipsan Beach in 1892.

Technically speaking, the initial lifesaving station organized in the Pacific Northwest was the North Cove station erected at the north entrance to Shoalwater Bay, in 1877. A skeleton tower and fixed light was built at Cape Shoalwater in 1858, and in 1941 a new 22,000 candlepower light was installed.

Urgent appeals for a lighthouse on Cape Disappointment received attention from the government in 1853. No place on the Pacific Coast needed a beacon more urgently than did the mouth of the Columbia. Plans were drawn for a high conical tower to stand 220 feet above the water as a permanent aid to navigation. When the funds were approved for the project, ships were dispatched to carry building materials from San Francisco.

American Bark *Oriole*

Laden with materials for the construction of the new lighthouse, the American bark *Oriole,* Captain Lewis Lentz, master, arrived off the mouth of the river, September 18, 1853.

The following day at dawn the vessel, then twenty-two days out of San Francisco, stood in for the crossing. The pilot boat came alongside and Pilot Flavel took command of the bark. Along about noon a southwest breeze arose and the vessel made slow headway, but two hours later the wind subsided and she dragged across the channel and struck the south sands in seventeen feet of water. The outgoing tide carried her seaward, banging her against the sand continually. The rudder was dislodged and water poured through her seams. The heavy machinery and construction material she carried caused her to settle deeper. Eventually the pumps became choked and the ship had to be abandoned.

The pilot took charge, owing to his familiarity with bar conditions. The boats were chained together and drifted throughout the night as the survivors tried in vain to keep warm. In all, the boats contained thirty-two persons many of whom were lighthouse construction men. Lentz had been the last to leave his ship, and none too soon, for fifteen minutes after he scrambled into the boat, the *Oriole* drifted off the spit, turned over on her beam ends, filled, and sank in six fathoms. Only a massive whirlpool was left on the bar.

The building materials were a total loss and the lighthouse construction faced further delay.

It was a happy group given to muffled cheers when the pilot schooner *California* hove in sight the following morning and rescued them. Pilot Flavel had earned the gratitude of Captain Lentz for his masterful skill in safeguarding the boats throughout the night.

The Cape Disappointment Lighthouse was finally completed in 1856, being one of the first permanent fixtures of its kind in the Pacific Northwest. It has been in constant service to the present year. The light stands high above the water and shines twenty miles to sea with a beam of 58,000 candlepower.

A lighthouse now non-existent was established at the northerly tip of Point Adams in 1875.

Heavy loss of life and property in the Pacific's Graveyard prompted the building of one of the most powerful lighthouses on the Pacific Coast in 1898. Built on North Head, this picturesque conical tower still stands today beaming out across the Pacific from an elevation of 194 feet. This light is visible for more than twenty miles at sea and operates with a beam of 260,000 candlepower.

The most fabulous of all the lighthouses in the Pacific's Graveyard, is the Tillamook Rock Light, located a mile and a half offshore from Tillamook Head. To construct this bastion, the top of the rock had to be dynamited to hollow a hole for its foundation. Completed in 1881, Tillamook Light has had a story that reads like fiction. It is situated several miles south of the river entrance, its primary purpose being to warn ships seeking entrance to the Columbia. The beacon glows from 134 feet above the ocean surface and is of 75,000 candlepower. In 1948, lack of Coast Guard funds almost forced the closure of the station, but an urgent appeal by commercial fishermen has kept the historic light in operation.

The *Columbia River Lightship*, twice removed from the original, is still very much a factor in the safe conduct of river traffic. In the spring of 1950, a new all-steel lightship costing $500,000 was completed at East Boothbay, Maine. She is to replace the forty-year-old

Columbia Lightship at the mouth of the river. The new vessel is 128 feet long.

The year 1885 was a banner year on the lower Columbia, for in April of that year construction got underway on the south jetty. The Government Harbor and River Bill of July, 1884, provided $100,000 for the work, but this was an inadequate sum for such an undertaking, and only 1000 feet of jetty were laid before the funds were exhausted.

More pressure was brought to bear on the government and in September, 1886, $187,500 in additional funds were expended for the project. This money was used to its best advantage, but the jetty was less than half completed when again the funds ran out. The rubble-mound jetty had taken shape, however, and the government now began to see its potentialities, and to realize the necessity of the undertaking. The result was the long awaited decision to allot $500,000 more for the project with additional amounts to be allocated until the job was finished.

The engineers got the green light to resume the work in the summer of 1888 and the lower river soon became a beehive of activity.

First a large receiving dock was constructed near Fort Stevens, and then came the rolling stock of five steam locomotives and sixty-five railroad dump cars. The sternwheel steamer *Cascades* was assigned the job of towing the barges between the up river quarry and Astoria. The tug *George H. Mendell* was engaged to continue the tow to Fort Stevens, where the rock was discharged, reloaded on the dump cars and pulled by locomotives on the trestle that extended over the jetty.

Log rafts arrived in large numbers for use in fortifying the trestle. Men from all walks of life were employed in the massive undertaking, and to accommodate them a fleet of mosquito launches were employed to carry workers to and from the job.

The estimated cost of the jetty was set by government officials at $3,800,000, but when the jetty was completed the total expenditure was only $2,025,000. It was one of the largest government projects of its kind in the United States at that period.

The jetty was nearly five miles long, and the entrance channels were dissolved into one deep passage when the last of the workers put away his tools in 1894. 2900 acres of surf became dry sand, and the channel deepened to thirty and thirty-five feet at low water.

Behind every great project are careful plans, and credit for the construction of the south jetty fell to G. B. Hegardt, superintendent; J. M. Stoneman, manager; and E. M. Philabaum, chief clerk.

.The jetty had accomplished the purpose, but in future years sand piled up at the opposite side of the river entrance which eventually necessitated the construction of a north jetty. The project was given consideration but the traditional red tape was encountered. Appropriations were finally allotted, and the U. S. Engineers built, between 1914 and 1916, a two-mile-long jetty which later included jetty A on the leeward side of the Cape. The north jetty ran toward the open Pacific over top of Peacock Spit.

The channel entrance was soon reduced to a width of about 2000 feet, and it steadily deepened until it afforded a splendid bar entrance.

Victory in the long battle against the elements at last appeared near.

Columbia River commerce officials were jubilant in the year 1925 when the annual bar survey made by the U. S. Army Corps of Engineers showed that the depth of water at the entrance to the river had deepened a minimum of one foot in all parts of the channel over the previous surveys and that the main ship channel had widened 800 feet during the year. The entrance to the river was then pronounced by the Engineers, "Eminently safe and easy of navigation."

The outcome of the survey was music to the ears of merchants and skippers, but the Pacific's Graveyard was yet to claim other victims.

Though the Columbia bar has maintained its project depth, the channel has not deepened to as great a depth as was originally predicted, and in 1949 an urgent appeal was made to deepen the entrance to a greater depth to assure safe passage at all times.

The present status of the bar was recently reflected by a plea from the Columbia River Bar Pilots Association, to deepen the channel to a depth of forty-eight feet. The pilots have complained that it is impossible to take large ships over the bar in rough weather without the danger of grounding.

It was surmised that the bar would deepen of its own accord to a depth of fifty feet after the jetties were completed, but this has not proved true. It is further estimated by some authorities that the proposed dredging of the bar entrance beyond its present project depth of forty feet would involve an expenditure of millions of dollars.

A project depth of forty feet has been maintained for twenty years, but the pilots say a more adequate bar is necessary for deep draft vessels. Bar recordings of 1949 showed forty-four feet of water on the entrance ranges, shoaling to forty feet on the Sand Island range, opposite Clatsop Spit, to thirty-five feet in Desdemona Channel, and thirty-four and a half feet on the Flavel and Tansy ranges.

Willapa Bay Bar

When Willapa bar was discovered, its shoal infested appearance deterred Meares from attempting to enter. It was surveyed in 1852 and 1855 by the U. S. Survey, under James Alden, who found that it had two entrances separated by a middle ground on which was an island, in a similar way to the entrance of the Columbia. In 1868 this arrangement was changed. The south channel had filled up and was said to be of little use, while the north channel had increased to a depth of five fathoms, and was much wider and deeper. The island had disappeared and some ships passed over the place where it had once existed.

No jetties have been constructed at the harbor entrance, but dredging has established a mean low water depth of twenty-three feet. Today there are two channels over the Willapa bar, one to the north and the other to the south. The latter is undependable and charts warn mariners to take every precaution if using this channel. Warning is also given that the shoals of the bar change at frequent intervals, necessitating a constant change of channel markers.

In 1855, Shoalwater, or Willapa Bay, at the south channel had four fathoms of water over it, and was a mile wide and two miles off the beach south of Leadbetter Point. Even then all ship masters were warned to stay clear of the area without the aid of a pilot, for the bay as its name implies, was full of shoals, and at low tide about one-half of the area was laid bare. Though good but narrow channels were found throughout its extent, they were lacking proper navigation instructions. Low water on the bay brought swift currents and dangerous eddies.

It is of interest to note that many of the early navigators considered Willapa bar far more easy of navigation than the Columbia bar, which doubtless was true until the gigantic program of conquering the Columbia's entrance was begun.

In 1950, funds were asked for dredging Willapa Channel to a project depth of twenty-six feet.

American Freighter *Mauna Ala*

The story of the *Mauna Ala* shows the necessity of aids to navigation and what happens when they become inoperative.

On December 7, 1941, the news of the Japanese bombardment of Pearl Harbor reached continental United States. Three days later the entire coast was blacked out. Under-sea marauders were taking their toll of American ships in the Pacific, and all radios were silenced.

The Matson Line Christmas ship *Mauna Ala* was en-route to Honolulu when she received a dispatch to return to the nearest port immediately. The vessel had received vague reports of the bombing of Pearl Harbor, but her officers were ignorant of the fact that the coast was under total blackout.

Several days later the following report on the loss of the *Mauna Ala,* was forthcoming from the Bureau of Inspection and Navigation:

"The blackout of navigation aids, lights and the silencing of radio beacons at the mouth of the Columbia River under wartime restrictions caused the wreck of the *Mauna Ala,* which stranded on Clatsop Spit, December 10, 1941."

At the hearing, O. S. Anderson, ship's officer of the wrecked freighter testified that thirty minutes before breakers were sighted, the *Mauna Ala* was ordered to halt by blinker light from a passing vessel. He stated that a light fog made it impossible for him to determine whether the third letter of the message was actually "L", but that the radio operator definitely believed the message to read "halt." Anderson further said that Captain C. W. Saunders, Jr., master of the freighter had been informed of the blinker warning and had accordingly ordered "dead slow " for several minutes, but later ordered full speed ahead, expecting momentarily to sight the lightship. Shortly after, breakers were sighted and the freighter piled up on the sands at 6 p.m., two and one half miles south of the position of the lightship. Observers on the beach said they could see the vessel's running lights before she hit the sands.

No one aboard the *Mauna Ala* was aware that the vessel was near the beach until she struck. She drove aground, her screw still spinning, and came to rest 700 feet from the shore. She pushed her bow hard on the sands and several hours later was turned broadside by the surf. It was then that the breakers began their destruction.

The Coast Guard lifeboats removed the crew of thirty-five and took them to Point Adams, while tugs and salvage craft stood by the freighter.

Lashed by high winds and heavy seas, the steamer broke in two several days later, most of her $750,000 cargo being lost. Besides the 60,000 Christmas trees, she carried a large shipment of turkeys, meats, general cargo, lumber and shingles. The holiday essentials were for Hawaii's Christmas from Pacific Northwest ports.

On December 17, the Columbia Salvage Company began operations to save parts of the ship's cargo, but the efforts were short lived.

Captain Saunders testified that the *Mauna Ala* was 750 miles at sea when orders were received to return to port. She carried no pilot and the proximity of land could not be determined when the ship went aground in the blackout.

The big freighter built at Bath, Maine, in 1918, as the *Canibas,* grossed 6,256 tons, and is one of the largest lost around the Columbia bar.

U. S. ARMY FERRY *ARROW*

CHAPTER ELEVEN

CONCLUSION

What becomes of the hulks rotting in the sands of the Pacific's Graveyard? Why do they disappear so quickly and how durable are the materials of which they are composed?

Wooden hulls survive the rigors longer than those of iron or steel construction when they become buried in the beds of sand or sink to the bottom of the ocean. It is hard to determine the length of time it takes for either to disintegrate completely, but it is known that wooden vessels have been dug up after centuries, not yet wholly decayed. It is not believed that iron or steel vessels can resist the elements for any great time due to the chemical effects of sea water.

When a wooden vessel sinks, the rate of progress to the bottom is very slow. It is not believed to be faster than 100 fathoms in fifteen minutes, unless it is laden with some weighty cargo such as coal or mineral ore. Thus when she touches bottom, especially if the material be mud or sand, the impact is gentle and no damage is done to the structure beyond what it received at the surface. Neither is there any mechanical agency to interfere with it. Currents are harmless, and the force of the waves ceases a comparatively few feet below the surface. So there the wreck lies practically in a quiet which will never be disturbed until the end of the world.

The action of sea water is not very rapid, either, and paint protects the shell and the metal work that holds it together. The wreck is gradually covered with barnacles and marine growth, layer upon layer until it is covered completely, while sea and river sediment slowly settles down over it. It is claimed that wrecked ships lying at the ocean bottom have been the beginning of a reef, shoal or similar obstruction.

When an iron or steel ship sinks, especially a steamer with heavy boilers and engines and a closely packed heavy cargo, it is apt to go down with great rapidity. Her collision with the ocean floor may go far to break her up.

Whatever happens, she has the corrosive effects of the salt water to withstand as well as all or most of the factors that affect the wooden ship. Vegetation settles on her wooden parts, and barnacles, teredos and other marine growth themselves are the cause of a chemical change. Every scratch in the paint is an opening for corrosion. Presently the paint itself scales off, and after many decades there will be little more than a rust stain at the bottom of the sea to mark where the vessel found her resting place.

It is interesting to note that of all of the vessels that have stranded on the shoals of the Pacific's Graveyard, the remains of about a half dozen show a vestige of themselves. Yet probably deep under the sands and off-shore, parts of old wrecks still remain intact. The bones of ships buried in this area have frequently been uncovered by the shifting sands along the beaches and then completely buried again within a short period of time. Offshore, areas of quicksand prevail and often ships have been doomed by settling on one of these quagmires.

The Pacific's Graveyard has also played host to many minor accidents, not fatal, but which have cost ship-owners thousands of dollars in repairs. Between 1910 and 1912, before the construction of the north jetty, more than thirty ships stranded or struck the sands of those shores, and damages ranged between $1000 and $15,000 per ship. Many of these vessels were heavily laden when they struck.

To estimate the amount of ship damage and total destruction in this area would be a difficult problem, but it is a known fact that it would run into the hundreds of millions of dollars, a far greater sum than has been expended to make the area safe for navigation.

Cape Disappointment has fittingly become the tombstone over this maritime cemetery. Standing as a massive bastion against the marauding swell of the ocean, it has witnessed a grim chapter to the chronicle of Pacific Northwest ship disaster. The sandy spits crowned with precipitous cliffs and beetling crags have provided a fit setting for the tragedies enacted here.

APPENDIX

BARK *ALICE*

APPENDIX A

*Appendix to ships that have stranded, foundered, burned, or
that have otherwise been lost in or around
the Pacific's Graveyard*

(vessels of 25 tons and over)

Abbey Cowper, British bark, 699 tons, stranded at Leadbetter
Point, near Shoalwater Bay, January 4, 1885. No lives were lost
in the wreck but the ship was a total loss. She was carried
ashore by the currents in a thick fog, while in command of
Captain William Ross. The wreck occured while the vessel
was enroute to Portland from Mollendo in ballast.

Admiral, American schooner, 605 tons, was driven into the
south jetty of the Columbia bar, January 13, 1912. The crew
were rescued but the vessel drifted across the river mouth
and capsized, becoming a total loss. See story page 57).

Admiral Benson, American steamship, 3,049 tons, stranded
near Buoy No. 6, near Peacock Spit, at the mouth of the Columbia, February 15, 1930. Passengers and crew were saved
but the vessel was totally wrecked. (See story page 124).

Alfa, American gas screw, 36 tons, wrecked near Ocean
Park, Washington, September 19, 1924. The craft was wrecked

143

while trying to land an illegal cargo of liquor on Klipsan Beach. The crew narrowly escaped with their lives and the vessel was leveled by the surf.

Alice, French ship, 2,509 tons, driven ashore in a gale one mile north of Ocean Park, at 4:10 a.m., January 15, 1909. The crew were rescued but the ship proved a total loss. She was bound for Portland from London with 3000 tons of cement consigned to Hind, Rolph & Company. She was commanded by Captain Aubert, and was 176 days at sea via Hobart, when misfortune overtook her. The *Alice* was built at Bordeaux, France, in 1901, and was one of the largest French vessels in operation to the Columbia. A vestige of the wreck was still visible in 1950, at extreme low tide. The last of her three masts tumbled into the sea in 1930.

Allegiance, British ship, stranded on Sand Island, in May, 1879. No lives were lost and the vessel was later refloated, repaired and returned to service.

Alsternixe, German bark, 3059 tons, stranded in heavy weather at dusk, February 9, 1903, one and one half miles southwest of Cape Disappointment Light. Complement of the vessel, including Captain Richard Auhagen, were rescued the following morning by the lifesaving crew. Several weeks later, the vessel was refloated after earlier having been considered a total loss. The four-masted bark, valued at $90,000, hailed from Hamburg, and was one of the few large ships to escape the sands of Peacock Spit. The stranding was attributed to the vessel getting out of the marked channel.

Americana, American schooner, 900 tons, went missing with all hands after clearing the Columbia bar, February 28, 1918. She was believed to have foundered in a gale, but no trace was ever found. The *Americana* was enroute to Sydney, Australia, from Astoria, with lumber.

Andrada, British bark, 1200 tons, vanished with all hands several miles west of the Columbia bar, December 11, 1900. She is believed to have foundered in a gale off the Washington Coast on December 15, but no trace of her has ever been found.

Anna C. Anderson, American schooner, vanished at sea with her party of seven men, under Captain W. H. Stapleford in January, 1869. The vessel was outbound from Oysterville with a cargo of oysters for San Francisco. She was last seen crossing Shoalwater bar. Speculation led to the master of the schooner having crowded on superfluous sail for a fast passage south due to the perishable cargo. The craft was perhaps struck by a heavy blow before her canvas could be taken in, causing her to capsize and sink. The vessel was owned by John and Thomas Crellin, of Oysterville and S. Morgan of San Francisco.

Architect, American bark, 279 tons, stranded on Clatsop Spit, March 28, 1875. She was in ballast from San Francisco enroute to Cementville on the Columbia. Following the ship *Pactolus* across the bar, the wind failed, causing her to go on the sands. After spending the night in the rigging in refuge from the surf, Captain Mertage and his crew were rescued by a lifeboat manned by Lieutenant Samuel Jones and the Allen Brothers of Astoria, who were towed to the scene of the wreck by the tug *Astoria.* F. C. Carr, of Astoria, purchased the wreck for $52, but salvaged little of value. The *Architect* was built at Rockland, Maine, in 1865, and was insured for $8,000 at the time of the wreck.

Ariel, American schooner, wrecked on Clatsop Spit in 1886. The crew is believed to have been saved. No record appears to have been kept as to which schooner *Ariel* was lost at the river mouth. It was claimed by some of the old timers to have been the 99-ton schooner *Ariel* built at Baltimore in 1853, and registered at San Francisco, and others say she was the 43-ton schooner-yacht *Ariel* built at New York in 1873, later becoming a unit of the Pacific sealing fleet.

Arrow, American steamship, 2,157 tons, wrecked at Cranberry Road, a few miles north of Long Beach, February 13, 1947. She parted her tow line and was carried ashore with nobody aboard. (See story page 76.)

Artemisia, American schooner or sloop, was wrecked south of Klipsan Beach in 1889. No lives were lost. The vessel was one of the early day units of the Shoalwater Bay mosquito fleet. She first made her appearance in the area in 1875, under Captain E. G. Loomis.

Aurelia, American steam schooner, 424 tons, stranded at Buoy No. 8, on the Columbia bar, August, 1911. The vessel was later refloated and repaired.

Aurora, American ship, 346 tons, stranded on the sands off Grays Bay inbound from San Francisco in June, 1849, in ballast. Aboard were twenty-six passengers all of whom were rescued by John Hobson on his flat barge from Astoria. The *Aurora* was skippered by Captain H. Kilbourn, formerly of the brig *Henry.* A short while after the passengers were rescued a gale arose and destroyed the vessel. All hands were saved. The ship was in quest of lumber for the return trip when disaster occurred. Built at Baltimore in 1823-24, the *Aurora* was owned throughout most of her career by Robert Kermit and James Mowatt of Baltimore, and was classed as a packet ship.

Barge unnamed, American, 1000 ton log capacity, went ashore near Long Beach, March 30, 1950. The unrigged vessel was owned by Sause Brothers of Garibaldi, Oregon. She went aground after breaking away from the tug *Klihyam* during a heavy gale. A second barge also got away in the rough seas, but the tug's crew managed to "lasso" it. The tug, also owned by Sause Brothers returned a week later and succeeded in pulling the barge off the beach. The salvage job was considered "remarkable" as most of the jobs of this kind have proved unsuccessful. Often times small fishing craft that go aground on the peninsula are dragged up the beach and hauled away on trucks.

Bordeaux, American brig, 250 tons, was wrecked on Clatsop Spit, December 13, 1852. The disaster occurred while the vessel was bound for San Francisco from Puget Sound. She ran into the Columbia River for an unscheduled call and fell victim to the currents when the wind died on the bar. The crew walked ashore on dry sand, but the vessel was later demolished in the surf.

Brodick Castle, British ship, 1,820 tons, disappeared with all hands after departing the Columbia River, December, 1908. She is believed to have foundered in a gale.

C. A. Klose, American schooner, 401 tons, drifted ashore bottom up on North Beach Peninsula, March 26, 1905. (See story page 56.)

Cairnsmore, British bark, 1,300 tons, stranded on Clatsop pit, September 26, 1883. All hands were rescued; the vessel was a total loss. (See story page 113.)

Canadian Exporter, Canadian steamship, 5400 tons, stranded in the fog on Willapa bar, August 1, 1921. No lives were lost but the freighter eventually broke in two. (See story page 121.)

Caoba, American steam schooner, 683 tons, wrecked north of Ocean Park, February 5, 1925. The crew abandoned her at sea. (See story page 64.)

Cape Wrath, British bark, 2,140 tons, vanished off the mouth of the Columbia River, January 16, 1901, with her crew of fifteen. The vessel was sighted off the river, seventy-five days out from Callao for Portland, and was never heard of thereafter. It is believed that she was a victim of a terrific storm that struck the area on the day she was last reported. The big bark was registered at Glasgow, and was owned by the Lyle Shipping Company.

Carrie B. Lake, American schooner, 36 tons, stranded near the present location of Long Beach, January 3, 1886. Three lives were lost, including Captain John Exon and two seamen. Two others struggled ashore in the surf. The schooner was built on Puget Sound in 1883, and was valued at $3,000. She was completely destroyed.

Cavour, Italian ship, 1,354 tons, stranded on the sands two miles south of Cape Disappointment Light, on the night of December 8, 1903. The twenty-two year old vessel had been at anchor on the bar awaiting favorable winds, when a strong breeze came up suddenly from the south and swept her ashore with anchors dragging. The tugs *Wallula* and *Tatoosh* were unable to free the vessel, but the lifesaving crew from Point Adams, rescued the complement of sixteen men and Captain Telemore Sofianos. The *Cavour* was the first Italian ship lost on the bar. She was owned by G. Bucelli and Domingo Loero of Genoa, and was valued at $15,000. The ship was built at Nova Scotia in 1881.

Challenger, American schooner, 279 tons, caught fire off the Oregon Coast and burned for several days until towed across Willapa bar and scuttled in the Willapa River, November 7, 1904. (See story page 98.)

Champion, American schooner, driven ashore on the north spit of the Columbia bar, April 15, 1870. The vessel was enroute to Shoalwater Bay from the Columbia River and was swept ashore by the currents when the wind failed while outbound. The six year old vessel, in command of Captain Dodge, was under charter to a Mr. Mudge of Astoria. After the schooner stranded she was swept on her beam ends and the crew took to the boat. The boat, however, swamped and they attempted to return to the wreck when a tremendous breaker struck and tossed them out of the boat. Two were drowned and the remaining survivor, an Indian, was carried to sea on the overturned lifeboat to which he had lashed himself. The following morning the boat and it's occupant were carried ashore on the North Beach Peninsula.

Chatham, His Majesty's Ship (tender) British, 135 tons,

stranded on what is now part of Peacock Spit, October 20, 1792, in command of Lieutenant William Broughton. Though the stranding was at first believed to be of a serious nature they got her off on the change of the tide.

Childar, Norwegian motorship, 4,138 tons, grounded on the southwest end of Peacock Spit, May 3, 1934. Four lives were lost but the freighter was pulled to safety in one of the most remarkable salvage feats of the decade. (See story page 91.)

City of Dublin, British ship, 814 tons, wrecked on Clatsop Spit, after the currents carried her on the shoal when the wind failed on the bar, October 18, 1878. The vessel was enroute to Portland from Port Chalmers, and was forty-nine days at sea. She was in command of Captain David Steven who, being unfamiliar with the landmarks, stood in too close to the bar, and was helpless to bring his ship about after the breeze failed. The anchor cables parted and the vessel was dashed hard on the sands. The crew made shore safely. Two weeks later salvage attempts were commenced but proved unsuccessful. The *City of Dublin* was valued at $40,000.

Columbia River Lightship No. 50, American, 296 tons, was carried ashore inside McKenzie Head at the north entrance of the Columbia, November 29, 1899. The crew was saved and several months later the vesel was refloated in one of the most interesting salvage feats ever performed. (See story page 84.)

Corsica, British bark, 778 tons, foundered twelve miles southwest of the Columbia bar, February 21, 1882. The vessel was bound for Queenstown, N.S.W., from Portland, with a full cargo of grain. She was drawing twenty feet when she passed over the bar in tow of the tug *Astoria.* The heavy swell caused her to strike the sands on three occasions and she commenced to take water rapidly. Captain W. H. Vessey, fearing for the lives of his wife and child, ordered the *Astoria* to come alongside and take them ashore, while the tug *Fearless* stood by. The pumps were manned continuously, but the vessel settled deeper and deeper. The *Fearless* tried to get a line on her, but Vessey refused to take it. At midnight the vessel had taken ten feet of water in her hold and the pumps were choked with wheat chaff. Finally she was abandoned and the crew rescued by the *Fearless.* The bark plunged to the bottom at 5 a.m. The cargo was valued at $50,000 and the vessel at $30,000. The *Corsica* was built in 1869.

Deneb, American, converted landing craft, enroute to

Alaska, was driven ashore four miles south of Ocean Park in May, 1950, when the main water pump failed. She was salvaged and towed to safety by the 3600 h.p. *Salvage Chief*, of Portland. The *Deneb's* master was John Niemi.

Desdemona, American bark, 331 tons, stranded on Desdemona Sands, so named after the wreck, January 1, 1857, with the loss of one life. (See story page 31.)

Detroit, American brig, 141 tons, stranded on the middle sands of the Columbia bar, after missing stays, on December 25, 1855. Later she drifted free but her bottom had been fouled and she took water rapidly. In twenty minutes, seven feet of water filled her hold, and the frightened crew refused to work. The brig's master lashed the wheel hard over and squared the sails and then gave the order to abandon ship. The men were picked up by the pilot boat *California* and taken to Astoria in time for Christmas dinner. The *Detroit* drifted about the mouth of the river for twenty-four hours, and was finally carried ashore near Tillamook Head. James Cook, a resident of Astoria, purchased the wreck and stripped her remains. At the time of the accident, the *Detroit* was enroute to San Francisco from Astoria. The eighty-four foot vessel was built at Guilford, Connecticut, in 1836.

Devonshire or *Dovenshire,* British, rig unknown, wrecked on Clatsop Spit in 1884. Very little is known concerning this wreck, but the vessel is said by some to have been an early British tramp steamer.

Dewa Gungadhar, British bark, 594 tons, went aground in the fog near Leadbetter Point, south of Shoalwater Bay, January 18, 1885. The bark was in command of Captain John Battersby, and was inbound for the Columbia River from Magdalena Bay. Over-running the Columbia entrance, she was trapped by the currents and carried northward. Despite the dropping of both anchors, the vessel dragged on to the beach and became a total loss. A rescue crew got a line on the wreck and rescued the thirteen men aboard.

Dilharree, British bark, 1,293 tons, met disaster while outbound from the Columbia bar in tow of two bar tugs. She carried a full grain cargo from Portland destined for Queenstown, N.S.W. In transit, the bark veered toward the shore and ran aground on the tip of Peacock Spit, March 10, 1880. The two tugs and a revenue cutter tried in vain to pull her to safety, but under her heavy load the vessel refused to oblige. The crew abandoned, and after a narrow escape in the boats was rescued. The composite vessel was valued at $65,000 and the cargo at $78,000. The respective skippers of the tugs were exonerated of blame when it was learned that the bark had failed to answer to her helm after the steering mechanism became jammed. The vessel was owned by John Lidgett, of London, and all the ships of his fleet had name prefixes beginning with "Dil," a Hindustani word meaning heart. The name *Dilharree,* for instance, meant "Heart's Delight."

Dolphin, American brig, omitted from records, was wrecked on Clatsop Spit in 1852, while attempting to enter the river. The vessel was carried on the beach and demolished, but the crew reached shore safely.

Douglas Dearborn, American schooner, 1,024 tons, was discovered bottom up several miles off the mouth of the Columbia River, January 4, 1890. No trace of her crew has ever been found. The vessel was totally destroyed.

Dovenshire, see *Devonshire.*

Drexel Victory, American steamship, 7,607 tons, foundered outside the Columbia entrance, one quarter mile due west of Buoy No. 6, January 19, 1947. The crew of forty-nine were all rescued. (See story page 107.)

Drumcraig, British bark, 1,979 tons, went missing with all hands enroute to Manila from Astoria in 1906. The iron vessel was last seen crossing the Columbia bar well freighted with a load of lumber. The 280-foot square rigger was built in 1885, and was owned by Gillison & Chadwick as a unit of the famous "Drum" fleet.

Edith Lorne, British bark, 805 tons, stranded on the middle sands of the Columbia bar, November 17, 1881. The vessel was bound for Queenstown, N.S.W., from Portland with a cargo of wheat. She was crossing the bar in company with the ship *Napier* when she brought up on the shoal. The stranding occurred with a pilot aboard. The vessel was in command of Captain William Watt. As she yawed on the sands, the bark's stern post cracked and the rudder was unshipped. Shortly the vessel began to break up. The Fort Canby surfboat crew, led by Captain Albert Harris maneuvered to the scene and rescued the ship's company. The vessel, which ultimately became a total loss, was valued at $58,000, and her cargo at $44,000. She was drawing eighteen feet of water when she struck the sands.

Efin, American, river freight boat, 196 tons, was destroyed by explosion and fire at 9:30 p.m. after departing Ilwaco for Astoria, May 11, 1937. The fire was caused by a fuel tank explosion. Capt. Alfred Babbidge and his crew of ten took to the lifeboat and were picked up half clothed by the motor lifeboat from Cape Disappointment. Among the crew was a woman cook. The *Efin* burned to the water's edge and her remains drifted to Sand Island. The vessel built at St. Helens, Oregon, in 1914, was owned by Babbidge & Holt, of Portland.

Electra, American fish boat, 72 tons, stranded on Clatsop Spit, inside the river bar, January 26, 1944. All hands were rescued. The Coast Guard cutter *Nemaha* attempted several times to pull the craft to safety, but was unsuccessful. A year later only the *Electra's* mast remained above the sand and surf.

Ellen, American schooner, wrecked on Shoalwater bar, April 20, 1870. The vessel was loaded with lumber when she was destroyed at the bar entrance. Her crew members were saved, after a narrow escape in the surf. The *Ellen* was a small coaster that was built for the Tillamook-Shoalwater Bay trade in 1865.

Emily Stevens, American schooner, 100 tons, stranded on Clatsop Spit, February 8, 1881. She was first given up as a total loss and abandoned by her crew, who were picked up by the tug *Columbia.* Later the schooner drifted off the shoal, and floated out to sea where it was picked up comparatively undamaged by the tug *Columbia,* which towed it to Astoria, and collected $950 in salvage money. Master of the tug was Captain Eric Johnson. The 87-foot schooner was built at Westport, Oregon, in 1879, by Captain Alexander Henderson for service as a halibut schooner. At the time the *Stevens* struck Clatsop Spit she was inbound from Eureka for Portland with a cargo of lumber.

Empire, American schooner, missed stays and stranded on the Shoalwater bar in 1854. The schooner was outbound for San Francisco from Oysterville well freighted with oysters. Her crew struggled to safety through the surf.

Fanny, American sloop, was dismasted and waterlogged off Shoalwater Bay, in 1864. Her crew took to the boats and were later picked up at sea. The wreck capsized and became a menace to navigation. Her remains were rammed and sunk by the steamship *Pacific.*

Fern Glen, British ship, 818 tons, was cast ashore on Clatsop Spit, when Captain F. Budd, her master, mistook Tilla-

mook Rock Light, for Point Adams Light, and ran his ship
on the beach at 4 a.m. October 16, 1881. The vessel was enroute to Portland in ballast from Wellington, New Zealand,
to load grain. The following day the twenty crew members
were employed in removing the ballast to lighten the vessel's
burden, but that evening a southwest gale arose and put the
vessel in a serious situation. The steamer *General Canby* attempted to rescue the seamen, but was prevented from getting near the wreck by the heavy surf. Later the ship began to
heel over when the ballast shifted, and the crew managed
to launch a damaged lifeboat, and row to the side of the tug
Columbia which was standing off the wreck. The *Fern Glen,*
a ship of graceful lines was classed as a medium clipper, and
was valued at $40,000. Captain Budd was criticized over the
loss of his ship as the accident occurred in perfect weather on
a starlight night.

Firefly, American steam tug, was carried ashore near Tansy
Point while towing logs at the mouth of the Columbia, February 24, 1854, with a loss of four lives. The tug was enroute
to Welsh's Sawmill from Young's River in command of Captain Thomas Hawks. As she rounded Smith's Point she was
met by a strong ebb tide and was unable to make any headway against the currents. Her low power engine could not
stand the strain and the tug was carried on the sands at Tansy
Point with her tow drifting aimlessly behind. Hawks refused
to cut his tow loose, fully expecting to get off on the next
tide. The mounting surf, however, carried the log raft ashore
and pulled the tug after it, causing her to capsize and sink,
taking the Captain and three crew members to a watery grave.
Aboard the tug was I. Welsh, owner of the mill for which
the logs were destined. He was thrown clear of the wreck and
managed to scramble up on the log raft. He succeeded in
severing the hawser with his knife and was carried all the way
to Astoria astride of the raft. When a salvage party returned
to the scene of the wreck only the tug's tall stack rose above
the surface, but to it they found clinging the tug's fireman,
whom they rescued. The stubby tug was brought to the
river from San Francisco only a year prior to her loss.

Fishing fleet, May 4, 1880. One of the most tragic events
that has occurred in the Pacific's Graveyard was the loss of
the entire fleet of fishing craft and the drowning of two-hun-
dred fishermen in 1880. The disaster occurred when the local
"small fry" fish boats from the Columbia and Shoalwater
Bay were fishing off the mouth of the Columbia. With no

advance warning, gale-like winds swept in from the southwest and turned the waters into angry chasms and mountainous swells. The helpless craft were overturned and swamped one after another and their contents swallowed in the tempest.

Francis H. Leggett, American steamship, 1,606 tons, foundered in a gale sixty miles southwest of the Columbia River September 18, 1914, with a loss of sixty-five lives. Only two were saved after a terrible ordeal in storm-tossed seas. The vessel carried a cargo of railroad ties, which several days later drifted ashore on the Tillamook and Nehalem beaches, along with some bodies. The revenue cutter *Bear,* the Japanese cruiser *Idzimno,* and the tanker *Frank Buck* answered the distress calls, but when they arrived at the scene, the *Leggett* had foundered. She was outbound from Grays Harbor for San Francisco. The steamer was built at Newport News in 1903 for the Hammond Lumber Company.

Frank W. Howe, American schooner, 573 tons, was carried ashore near Seaview, just north of North Head, February 22, 1904, after becoming waterlogged at sea. (See story on page 55.)

G. Broughton, British bark, 803 tons, stranded at Leadbetter Point just south of the entrance to Shoalwater Bay, November 1, 1881. The vessel, inbound for Portland from Brisbane, Australia, was in ballast, and struck the beach at night in thick weather. Off the mouth of the Columbia the vessel had drifted northward with the prevailing currents before taking to the beach. Captain Payne, ordered the masts chopped down in an effort to lighten the vessel, but she failed to relinquish her place in the sands, and the crew of sixteen had to be rescued. She remained on an even keel for three days and then careened over and dug her grave in the sands. The vessel was owned by Peter Iredale & Porter of Liverpool, and was valued at $40,000. She grounded one day after the *Lammerlaw* went ashore in almost the identical spot, and both ships became total losses within a few feet of one another.

Galena, British bark, 2,294 tons, stranded on Clatsop Beach at night, on November 13, 1906. She was inbound from Junin, Chile, in ballast to load grain at Portland. The weather had been severe and the vessel was beating off the mouth of the river waiting opportunity to pick up a pilot. She got in too close to shore and was carried on the beach by the surf. Captain Howell, and two of his officers stood by the vessel in hopes of salvaging her, but with the storm season coming on, the sands built up around the hull of the 292 foot steel vessel, and salvage prospects were abandoned. A few years later the ship was devoured by the sands. She was one of the largest and finest of the grain fleet and was owned by S. Galena & Company of Liverpool, for whom she had been built at Dundee in 1890.

General Warren, American steamship, 400 tons, ran aground on Clatsop Spit, in sinking condition, January 28, 1852. Forty-two lives were lost when the vessel was leveled by the surf. (See story page 47.) The *Warren* was built for the Portland Steam Packet Company, of Portland, Maine, in 1846, as one of the early propeller steamers seen in Maine. She came to the west coast during the California Gold Rush, and eventually entered coastwise service.

It is interesting to note that in October, 1854, two years after the *Warren* was lost, the whole stern frame of the vessel was found on the beach sixty miles to the north of the wreck—an example that shows the prevailing littoral current around the Columbia Bar.

Gleaner, American, river steamer, capsized off Tongue Point, enroute to Astoria from Deep River, at 11 a.m. January 28, 1888. The loss was caused by a gale that swept the lower river. The cargo shifted and the craft heeled over drowning one man and two women passengers. The remaining twenty-seven passengers took refuge in a fishing boat that the steamer was towing. The *Gleaner* was commanded by Captain Peter Jordan. The vessel was a propeller steamer that was built at Grays Bay in 1883.

Glenmorag, British ship, 1,567 tons, stranded north of Ocean Park, March 18, 1896, with the loss of two lives. (See story page 115.) The vessel was built in 1876, for the J. & A. Allen fleet.

Governor Moody, American pilot schooner, 65 tons, was wrecked at North Head, September 20, 1890. The crew were saved but the vessel was a total loss. (See story page 112.)

Grace Roberts, American barkentine, 286 tons, stranded two miles south of Leadbetter Point, December 8, 1887, without loss of life. The vessel, commanded by Captain M. Larsen, was feeling her way along the coast in a thick fog when she drifted into the breakers, knocking several holes in her hull. The crew had to take to the boats. Shipbreaker Martin Foard, purchased the wreck for a small sum and salvaged

the cargo and equipment. The *Roberts* was built at Port
Orchard, Washington, in 1868, at a cost of $30,000. It was
said that the owners of the barkentine had run the vessel
hard, overlooking badly needed hull repairs which may have
caused her to bilge on the sands. Parts of her barnacle en-
crusted remains could be seen on the peninsula as late as
1950. They are the oldest visible ship's remains in the Pacific's Graveyard.

Great Republic, American sidewheel passenger steamer,
4,750 tons, stranded on Sand Island, April 19, 1879. The passengers were safely evacuated, but eleven crew members were
drowned in the last full lifeboat to clear the wreck. (See
story page 35.)

Harvest Home, American bark, stranded four miles north
of North Head, January 18, 1882, without loss of life. The
vessel was beyond salvage. (See story page 111.)

Henrietta, omitted from records, was said to have been a
French bark that stranded on the south side of the river entrance near Astoria, in 1860.

Henriette, French bark, 735 tons, grounded on a reef of
rocks just above Astoria, on the south side of the river in a
gale on December 27, 1901. She settled on both anchors, which
forced a hole in her bottom, causing her to sink. Her master
filed suit against the crew of the tug *Walulla* for leaving him
at anchor when he was told that the bar was all right for
crossing. The twenty-seven year old iron vessel was salvaged
several months later and purchased by Simon McKenzie, for
use as a barge. Later she was converted to a steamer, and
then to a four-masted schooner. During her career she flew
the flags of France, the United States and England. The
vessel was lost in the South Seas in 1922.

I. Merrithew, American bark, stranded on Clatsop Spit,
January 12, 1853. She arrived off the Columbia December 30,
1852, after a twelve day passage from San Francisco, and due
to unfavorable conditions was compelled to stand off the
river several days. When no pilot came by January 11, Captain Samuel Kissam started his command across the bar. When
abreast of the red channel marker near Clatsop Spit, the
wind died and the bark was swept on the middle sands
dragging both anchors. The masts were cut away and the
cargo was jettisoned in an attempt to get her afloat. A gale
was in the making and was soon lashing at the wreck with
all its fury. The pilot boat set out from Astoria to rescue the

crew but was unable to do so until the following morning. Lying abandoned on the shoal, the *Merrithew* floated free and drifted seaward only to be caught in a cross current and swept into the rocks near North Head. At the time of the wreck, the vessel was carrying 128 tons of general merchandise.

Industry, American bark, 300 tons, stranded on the middle sands at the Columbia's entrance, March 15, 1865, with a loss of seventeen lives. (See story on page 33.)

Iowa, American steamship, 5,724 tons, stranded and foundered off Peacock Spit, January 12, 1936, with the loss of her entire crew of thirty-four. (See story page 71.)

Isabella, British bark, stranded on Sand Island, May 23, 1830, without loss of life. (See story page 24.)

J. C. Cousins, American pilot schooner, stranded on Clatsop Spit, October 7, 1883. No trace of her crew of four was ever found. (See story page 105.)

Jane A. Falkenberg, American barkentine, 310 tons, stranded on Clatsop Spit in 1872. At first it was feared that she would be lost, but determined salvage efforts went rewarded, and the vessel was eventually refloated from her sandy perch. She was built at New Bedford in 1854, and came to the Pacific Coast the following year. She had clipper lines and seldom made a slow passage. Shortly after her arrival on the coast she was purchased by Captain George Flavel.

Japanese Junk, unnamed, drifted ashore on Clatsop Spit in 1820, after being carried across the Pacific Ocean with the prevailing current. The vessel was denuded of life. (See story page 13.)

Jennie Ford, American barkentine, wrecked on a rocky shelf off North Head, January 29, 1864. The vessel was beating up the coast in command of Captain McCarty, and was enroute to Puget Sound from San Francisco in ballast. Out of the thick weather suddenly loomed a rocky promentory, and the vessel struck on the shelving undersea extension. She immediately began to break up, and the crew experiencd difficulty in launching the boat. A passenger named Osgood, was swept overboard and drowned. After several hours in an open boat the ship's party landed on North Beach, exhausted from their tribulations.

Jenny Jones, American schooner, stranded on Peacock Spit, May 14, 1864, while entering the river. The vessel and her party were miraculously saved. (See story page 79.) Shortly after the *Jenny's* escape from the shoals she was fitted out with a steam engine.

Jessie Nickerson, American schooner, 184 tons, was wrecked at the entrance to Shoalwater Bay in 1880. The schooner was commanded and principally owned by Captain Samuel Bonnifield of San Francisco. No lives were reported lost in the wreck. The *Nickerson* was constructed by the Hall Brothers yard at Port Ludlow, Washington, in 1874, and shortly before her loss had a fine passage to her credit of ten days from Honolulu to Humboldt Bay, California.

Josephine, British brig, wrecked on Clatsop Spit, in 1849. Very little is known of this wreck except that the vessel was totally destroyed. Some sources claimed she was of British registry, others French registry. No mention of loss of lives is made.

Kake, gas propelled salmon packer, American, 34 tons, was swept on the spit at midnight near the south jetty of the Columbia bar, November 1, 1913. The craft was destroyed in the surf but the crew was rescued. The *Kake,* commanded by Captain Morzey, was inbound from Kake, Alaska, with 360 cases of packed salmon. She was owned by the Sanborn-Cutting Company of Astoria.

Lammerlaw, British bark, 746 tons, stranded at Leadbetter Point, when her master, Captain Pringle, mistook Shoalwater bar for the Columbia bar, October 31, 1881. The vessel was bound for Portland from Newcastle, N.S.W., with a cargo of coal when she grounded. The lifesaving crew picked up the survivors, while the beachcombers picked up the coal to heat their homes. The officers' mess table and some silver service from the *Lammerlaw* is still in use at the home of Mr. and Mrs. Charles Nelson of Nahcotta. The bark was an iron vessel valued at $70,000, and was less than three years old at the time of the wreck. Captain Pringle was censured by the Board of Inquiry over the loss of his command.

Laurel, American steamship, 5,759 tons, stranded on Peacock Spit, June 16, 1929, with the loss of one life. (See story page 68.)

Lupatia, British bark, 1,300 tons, struck the shore and foundered off Tillamook Head, January 3, 1881, with the loss of her entire complement of 16 men. A dog was the only survivor. (See story page 51.)

Machigone, American schooner, disappeared with her crew of nine off the mouth of the Columbia, after departing Astoria for San Francisco, November 20, 1852. The windjammer, commanded by Captain I. H. Simpson put out from Astoria with a heavy load of lumber and shortly after her departure a terrible gale roared across the latitudes of the Columbia's mouth.

Maine, American ship, 300 tons, was wrecked on Clatsop Spit, in 1848. She was a whaler from the north Atlantic in quest of whales, when disaster overtook her. The crew was saved. John Hobson, of Astoria, secured rights to the wreck and recovered sufficient materials to open his own copper shop. The survivors tried in vain to book passage home, but no ship was available. Thus they purchased a ship's boat, lengthened and equipped it with sail and set out for San Francisco, where upon their arrival they signed on another ship for the passage home.

Makah, American barkentine, 699 tons, found bottom up off Tillamook Head, October 24, 1888, eighteen days after leaving Port Discovery, Washington, for Sydney, Australia, with lumber. No sign of her crew of eleven was ever found and the remains of the six year old vessel were rendered a total loss. She was commanded by Captain Larsen.

Marie, American brig, was wrecked in a fog two miles north of Cape Disappointment, November 29, 1852, with the loss of nine lives. The brig was enroute to Shoalwater Bay from San Francisco. The fog blotted out all landmarks and the vessel's master was unaware of the proximity of the shore until breakers were sighted and the vessel carried on the shoals. A boat was put over the side but immediately swamped, drowning its occupants. By the following morning the *Marie* was reduced to a total wreck and nine men, including the captain were dead. Two survivors struggled through the surf to safety and were later found on the beach suffering from exposure.

Mauna Ala, American steamship, 6,265 tons, stranded during the coastal blackout off Clatsop Beach, December 10, 1941. All hands were saved. (See story page 136.)

Melanope, British bark, 1,624 tons, dismasted and capsized in a storm in December, 1906. Abandoned at sea by her crew, the derelict was later picked up off the mouth of the Columbia by the steamer *Northland.* (See story, page 60.)

Mindora, American bark, stranded off Sand Island, without loss of lfe, January 12, 1853. (See story, page 29.)

Morning Star, French bark, stranded off Sand Island, with a loss of one life, July 11, 1849. (See story, page 27.)

Nabob, British bark, disappeared with her entire crew after crossing the Columbia bar, outbound with grain for the United Kingdom March 4, 1876. She was commanded by Captain Fetherstone.

Neptune, American, diesel tug, 415 tons, struck by the steamship *Herald of the Morning,* while maneuvering in to get a line on the vessel nine miles off the Columbia River, November 16, 1948. The *Neptune* was aiding in the towing of the freighter to Puget Sound from San Francisco, and the collision occurred in rough seas after the big steamship broke loose from the tug *Sea Fox.* The *Neptune* attempted to retrieve the tow. Her big tanks were punctured in the subsequent collision and shortly after she plunged to the bottom. The Coast Guard cutter *Balsam* picked up the survivors. One of the tug's crew died of a heart attack from immersion in the icy waters. The *Neptune* was a unit of the Puget Sound Tug and Barge Company, and was skippered by Captain Kelly Sprague.

Nimbus, American ship, 1,302 tons, struck the sands of the Columbia bar outward bound, and plunged to the bottom twenty-five miles northwest of the river, December 29, 1877. The vessel under pilot Thomas Doig, crossed the bar at 8:30 a.m. with a cargo of wheat from Portland valued at $92,500. Following the south channel, the ship scraped over the middle sands. When the pilot departed the ship, Captain R. L. Leonard discovered his vessel was taking water at an alarming rate. The vessel was put about and headed for shore, but the wind died and she was becalmed. Leonard signalled the *Aberystwith Castle* and the *Pilgrim* to stand by. At 7 p.m. when the water reached the tween decks of the *Nimbus,* the crew abandoned and was picked up by the stand-by sailing vessels. The ship went down a few hours later. She was valued at $65,000, and had been built at Bath, Maine, in 1869.

Nisqually, American barge, 1,251 tons, stranded on Clatsop Spit after breaking loose from the tug *Tyee* off the mouth of the Columbia, in March, 1938. The steel barge went ashore with 600,000 feet of peeler logs. The surf washed the deckload off the barge. Several weeks later salvage efforts proved successful and the craft was refloated. The barge, owned by Hubble Towing Company of Aberdeen, was the former steamship *Suremico,* built at Newark, New Jersey, in 1920. On June 3, 1927, she collided with the French freighter *Arkansas* off

Cape Flattery, Washington, and was so badly damaged that she was reduced to the role of a barge.

North Bend, American schooner, 981 tons, stranded on Peacock Spit, January 5, 1928, without loss of life. Thirteen months later she refloated herself. (See story, page 90.)

Orbit, American bark, stranded on Sand Island inbound from Puget Sound, March, 1850. Captain T. Butler and his crew, fearing that the breakers would make short work of the brig, abandoned her. Some Astorians with an eye for salvage later boarded the vessel and after herculean efforts succeeded in getting her afloat. She drifted to Bakers Bay, and was safely anchored. Michael Simmons, of Newmarket, Washington, paid off the salvagers and regained his vessel.

Orient, American brig, 324 tons, was wrecked at the south entrance to Shoalwater Bay, near Point Leadbetter, May 7, 1875. No lives were reported lost. The brig hailing from Boston, was operated in the coasting trades at the time of her loss.

Oriole, American bark, destroyed on the sands off Clatsop Spit, September 19, 1853. (See story, page 130.)

Oshkosh, American motor vessel, 145 tons, struck bottom off the south jetty of the Columbia bar, on February 13, 1911, with a loss of six lives. The vessel departed Tillamook for the Umpqua River, but ran into a strong southeast gale. Her fresh water tanks became filled with sea water, and Captain Latham, reversed his course and headed for the Columbia. The bar was in a disturbed condition for a crossing, and at 5 a.m., February 13, the vessel was tossed ashore and a few minutes later capsized carrying six of the seven men aboard to their deaths. The one survivor struggled up on the jetty rocks and was found by the lifesaving crew blue with cold. His name was George May. The *Oshkosh* was owned by the Elmore Navigation Company and had been carrying freight out of Astoria to other bar ports prior to her loss.

P. S. B. & D. Co. No 14, American scow, 142 tons, foundered off the mouth of the Columbia River, November 15, 1943. The scow was built in 1913, and owned by the Puget Sound Bridge and Dredging Company.

P.T. & B. Co. No. 1684 and *P.T. & B. Co. No. 1685,* American barges, 1007 tons each, were being towed to Honolulu from the Columbia River by the tug *Teton* of the Portland Tug & Barge Company, of Portland, Oregon. The barges were each loaded with $70,000 cargoes of lumber. Off the

mouth of the river heavy seas and high winds carried the
tug and barges toward Peacock Spit, and in order to save
the tug, the hawser had to be cut. Both barges went on
the spit January 18, 1947. The surf made kindling of the
cargo and the barges were a total loss. One of the barges was
swept against the rock walls of North Head. The owners of
the tug were exonerated in a $150,000 lawsuit involving the
lost cargo.

Palos, American brig, stranded on Leadbetter Point, at the
south entrance to Shoalwater Bay, in November, 1853. The
vessel was enroute to Oysterville from San Francisco, and
attempted to enter the bay in a thick fog. When the crew
and passengers were abandoning the ship, the captain was
swept overboard and drowned. The others reached shore
safely, but the vessel was pounded to pieces.

Peacock, U. S. Naval brig (Sloop of War) 275 tons,
stranded on Peacock Spit, July 18, 1841, without loss of life.
(See story, page 125.)

Pescawha, American motor schooner, 93 tons, was carried
into the north jetty and demolished, February 27, 1933, with
the loss of her master. (See story, page 67.)

Peter Iredale, British bark, 2,075 tons, stranded on Clatsop
Beach, October 25, 1906, with no loss of life. (See story, page
42.)

Point Loma, American steam schooner, 310 tons, grounded
on the North Beach Peninsula, near Seaview, February 28,
1896. In charge of Captain Conway, the vessel was enroute
to San Francisco from Grays Harbor with lumber. The day
prior to the wreck, one of the worst gales of that year struck
the steamer and at midnight the engines broke down and
water leaked into her hull and extinguished the fires in the
boilers. The wind and high seas carried the ship toward the
shore. Distress signals shot from her bridge were sighted by
shore lookouts, and the Fort Canby lifesaving crew hustled
down the beach to render aid. They launched a surf boat on
several occasions but each time it was repelled by the breakers. Finally a line shot from the beach reached its mark. The
crew of the wrecked steamer made it fast and then by means
of a raft were successful in getting ashore without the loss of
a man. Seventeen in all were saved. The vessel was pounded
to pieces. The *Point Loma* was built at San Francisco in 1888,
and was one of the pioneer steam schooners to engage in
coastwise lumber trades. She was last owned by the Grays

Harbor Commercial Company. Her remains could be seen on the beach at low tide until a few years ago.

Poltalloch, British bark, 2,250 tons, stranded on Shoalwater bar, November 26, 1900, without loss of life. She was eventually refloated. (See story, page 87.)

Potomac, American brig, wrecked on the Columbia bar, near the middle sands, in early May, 1852, outbound for San Francisco with lumber. The cargo was jettisoned after the vessel struck and she bumped the shoals constantly for several hours. Finally she drifted free and was carried to Astoria with the tide and currents. There she was surveyed and pronounced a total constructive loss. Her master was Captain Addison Drinkwater.

Potrimpos, German bark, stranded on North Beach Peninsula, near Long Beach, December 19, 1896, without loss of life. (See story, page 117.)

Primrose, wrecked on Clatsop Spit in 1882. Practically nothing is known concerning this wreck.

Queen of the Pacific, American passenger steamship, 2,727 tons, stranded on Clatsop Spit, September 5, 1883. In an all-out salvage effort utilizing the services of a fleet of tugs the liner was refloated. (See story, page 82.)

Republic, American shark boat, 25 tons, foundered off the mouth of the Columbia River, February 7, 1945, with the loss of her crew of four. Built in 1926, the vessel was a veteran of the Pacific Northwest fishing fleet.

Ricky, American fish boat, 25 tons, dragged anchor and was smashed against the rocks of the north jetty of the Columbia Bar, in a storm, July 22, 1949. Skipper J. B. Price and his crew fortunately escaped death.

Rival, American bark, 299 tons, stranded on Peacock Spit, September 13, 1881, and became a total loss. With a pilot aboard, the vessel was outbound for San Francisco loaded with hay and shingles from Knappton. While on the bar the wind died, and after a lull changed to an easterly direction. The bark drifted on the sands with both anchors dragging. The pilot schooner, near by at the time, summoned the tug *Astoria.* The tug managed to get a line on the wreck several hours later, but while attempting to pull the *Rival* free, it parted. Shortly after, the starboard anchor cable broke, and the vessel swung abruptly about. The tug was unable to get another line on the wreck and at 1:30 p.m. September 13, the *Rival* parted her port anchor chain and was carried high on the beach between Cape Disappointment and McKenzie Head. Captain Thomas B. Adams, the *Rival's* master, his wife and the crew, took to the boats and landed safely on the beach. The bark was valued at $8000, and her cargo at $6000. The vessel was regarded as a veritable floating coffin, her hull being old and tender. She was a total loss.

Robert Bruce, American schooner, was burned to the water's edge by a mutinous crew at Bruceport, on Shoalwater Bay, December 16, 1851. As told in the pages of Samuel Snowden's *History of Washington*, "The small but exceedingly palatable oysters for which Shoalwater Bay has since become noted, had been found, and during the summer of 1850, Captain J. W. Russell, had taken a small quantity of them to San Francisco by steamer, where they were received with much favor. Captain Felstead, also took a supply by sailing ship, but they arrived in bad order and were a total loss. Anthony Ludlam, then fitted out the schooner *Sea Serpent* to engage in the oyster trade, and a company was formed later which sent the schooner *Robert Bruce* to the bay for cargo, but while she was loading, the crew quarreled, and the ship was set on fire and burned to the water's edge. The crew being unable to get away, became permanent setlers, near what has since been known as Bruceport, from the name of the ship."

Rochelle, American steamship, 831 tons, wrecked on Clatsop Spit, near Buoy No. 12, October 21, 1914. On May 5, 1908, the steamer *Minnie E. Kelton* was towed to Astoria partially submerged, after having been buffeted by a storm that claimed eleven crew members off Yaquina Head, Oregon. At Astoria, the damaged vessel was stripped of her housing and used as a rock barge for the maintenance of the Columbia River jetty. Several months later she was rebuilt into a passenger steam schooner and renamed *Rochelle*. Ironically, the jetty which the vessel had helped maintain was the location of her loss. The steamer struck Clatsop Spit at night in thick weather. The engineer reported that the vessel was taking water fast and accordingly distress signals were shot into the air, which alerted the lifesaving crews at Point Adams and Cape Disappointment. The bar tug *Wallula* also rushed to the wreck. Captain Simon Kildahl, pilot H. A. Matthews, and the crew of nineteen were rescued by the Coastguardsmen. An hour later, the action of the breakers caused the steamer's cargo of coal to catch on fire and the wreck became a torch. By morning she was on the bottom with only a few charred timbers breaking the surface. At the time of the wreck the *Rochelle* was inbound to Portland from Boat Harbor, B. C. The twenty year old vessel was valued at $40,000. The pilot blamed the stranding on inoperative channel lights.

Rose Ann, American fish boat, 51 tons, disappeared with her crew of four somewhere off the mouth of the Columbia River in February, 1848. (See story, page 77.)

Rosecrans, American tanker, 2,976 tons, wrecked on Peacock Spit, with a loss of thirty-three lives, January 7, 1913. (See story, page 62.)

Rose Perry, schooner, went aground on the south spit of Shoalwater bar, in September, 1872. The vessel operated in the coasting trades at the time she was lost. Some sources claim that she was of Canadian registry.

Rudolph, American fish boat, 27 tons, stranded on Peacock Spit, September 2, 1945, without loss of life. The gas propelled vessel was built in 1911.

S. D. Lewis, American brig, stranded on Clatsop Spit, March 16, 1865, without loss of life. The vessel missed stays and went hard aground. She temporarily drifted free, but as the prow swung into the wind, a giant breaker carried her higher on the shoal. The crew took to the boats and managed to land in the surf. The brig eventually fell to pieces.

Sea Thrush, American steamship, 5,538 tons, stranded on Clatsop Spit in a heavy fog, December 4, 1932. The vessel was inbound from Puget Sound to complete loading for east coast ports. While groping her way without the aid of a bar pilot she struck the sands. Commanded by Captain Ernest J. Landstrom, the freighter carried a crew of thirty-one, but added to this total was a youthful stowaway and a woman passenger. The cutter *Redwing* and the Coast Guard motor lifeboats came to the rescue and removed all but the ship's master, the day after the ship stranded. On December 6, the freighter's keel snapped and she buckled amidships. Late that same day the Point Adams lifeboat made a daring run to the wreck and removed Captain Landstrom. On December 8, the vessel broke in two and became a total loss. The *Sea Thrush,* owned by the Shepard Steamship Company, was built at Portland, Oregon, by the Northwest Steel Company in 1917, as the initial vessel of the U. S. Shipping Board fleet constructed on the Pacific Coast. Her original name was *Westland,* a title suggested by Mrs. Woodrow Wilson, then first lady of the land.

Shark, U. S. Naval Survey schooner, 300 tons, stranded on Clatsop Spit, September 10, 1846, outbound from the river. The vessel was in command of Captain Schenck, and was part of the surveying fleet under Lieutenant Neil M. Howison, U.S.N. The *Shark* arrived on the Columbia after a twenty-five day passage from Honolulu in August, 1846, and while in transit to Astoria picked up a negro cook named Saul, who was a survivor of the *Peacock* disaster. He took over the piloting duties, but twenty minutes later ran the vessel on the sands. Fortunately the bar was calm and the *Shark* drifted free and bar pilot John Lattie was summoned to guide the schooner to safe waters. Anxiety over the boundary question involving the United States and Great Britain started rumors among the settlers that trouble was near and that the arrival of the *Shark* was a war precaution and not a survey mission. The crew members of the schooner, weary from long months at sea, began deserting and replacements were unobtainable. Thus the survey was rushed and the vessel hastily departed the river on September 10, without taking proper precautions. When she struck the shoal, her three masts were chopped down and her twelve cannon were jettisoned in an effort to get her off the spit. Instead she began to break up and the crew was forced to take to the boats. During the night the battered wreck drifted to sea and later

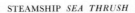

STEAMSHIP *SEA THRUSH*

came ashore just south of Tillamook Head. Among the wreckage was one of the Shark's cannon, which later was responsible for the naming of Cannon Beach, Oregon. This same cannon has been erected as a monument where many tourists still view it. John Hobson dismantled the wreck and the company of the *Shark* later sailed to San Francisco on the schooner *Cadboro* of the Hudson's Bay Company. A grim reminder of the loss of the vessel is Shark Rock, which stands in an Astoria city park. The survivors of the wreck inscribed the incident on the rock, which is still legible today. Howison claimed the wreck was due to channel alterations from the charts the *Shark* carried. He presented the ship's colors to the Astor Colony.

Solano, American schooner, 728 tons, stranded five miles north of Ocean Park, February 5, 1907. (See story, page 119.)

Spanish vessel, name unknown, stranded on Clatsop Beach, supposedly in the year 1725, years before the Columbia River had been discovered by white man. (See story, page 10.)

State of Washington, American sternwheel river steamer, 605 tons, destroyed by terrific explosion, June 23, 1920, off Tongue Point. The steamer was enroute to Portland, towing *oil barge No. 93* from Astoria. Suddenly she was shaken by a terrific boiler explosion and six members of the crew were seriously injured and another scalded to death. The sternwheeler was so completely demolished that all that kept her remains afloat was the hawser that remained fast to the oil barge. Nearby vessels came to the rescue and removed the injured men. The steamer was valued at $40,000. Her master was Captain H. L. Hill, but the vessel was in charge of the river pilot who had relieved the skipper a few minutes before the explosion occurred. The *State of Washington* was built at Tacoma in 1889, and was one of the best known sternwheel steamers in the Pacific Northwest.

Strathblane, British ship, 1,300 tons, wrecked south of Ocean Park, November 3, 1891, with a loss of seven lives. (See story, page 53.)

Sulphur, H.M.S. (British Naval Ship), 300 tons, stranded on Peacock Spit, while inbound on a surveying mission in 1839. No lives were lost and the ship was eventually refloated. The spot where she grounded was for many years known as Sulphur Spit. She was commanded by Captain Edward Belcher.

Sunshine, American schooner, 326 tons, drifted ashore bottom up on North Beach Peninsula, November 22, 1875. To this day no trace has been found of her party of twenty-five. (See story, page 103.)

Sylvia de Grasse, American packet ship, grounded on a ledge of rock off Astoria, in 1849. The ship was at anchor awaiting a pilot after loading a full cargo of lumber at up river ports. When the pilot boarded, the ship weighed anchor. The crew was aloft preparing to drop the canvas, when the ship drifted into a ledge of rock and remained fast. It appeared that she would be refloated within a few hours, but the vessel was overloaded with lumber and the cargo suddenly shifted causing her to wedge herself tighter on the rocks. With each passing day it became more evident that she could not be freed, and her owner William Gray who had voyaged on his ship from New York, attempted to shift his lumber to another craft so that it would arrive in San Francisco in time to collect the inflated Gold Rush prices. He offered the Captain of the American ship *Walpole* at anchor off Astoria, $10,000 to make the passage, but was refused as his ship was under charter to the United States Government. In desperation, Gray secured the services of three small schooners, and distributed the lumber between them. When the vessels arrived at San Francisco, Gray was informed that the lumber market had taken a drastic drop, and what might have been a successful venture ended in financial failure. The *Sylvia de Grasse,* a vessel of ancient vintage was claimed to have brought the first news of the French Revolution to the United States. Forty-five years after she was wrecked an Astoria boat builder visited the scene and removed some of her timbers, which he placed in the boat he was building. The old packet had been built of durable wood, mainly live oak and locust, unsurpassed for ship construction. Parts of her anchor chain are on display at the Oregon Historical Society.

Telephone, American sternwheel river steamer, 386 tons, caught fire and was beached north of Astoria, November 20, 1887. One life was lost in the conflagration. (See story, page 95.)

Tillamook, American sloop, see: Unknown sloop of 1876.

Tonquin, American ship, 269 tons, stranded momentarily on the Columbia bar while crossing inbound March 22, 1811. Due to the captain's haste to cross the bar before a heavy sea had abated, he sent several of his men needlessly out to sound the bar in small boats. Eight of them were drowned. (See story, page 15.)

Trinidad, American steam schooner, 974 tons, stranded on the north spit of Willapa bar between Buoys 6 and 7, May 7, 1937. One life was lost. (See story, page 72.)

U. S. Grant, American steamer, 47 tons, broke loose from her moorings and was totally wrecked after grounding on Sand Island, December 19, 1871. (See story, page 50.)

Unknown sloop of 1876, was wrecked on Clatsop Beach in February, 1876, with the loss of her entire crew. The vessel was built new in that year at Tillamook, Oregon, and was commanded by Captain William Terwilliger, who was also her owner. Seven persons, including two eight-year-old boys were drowned when the vessel was cast into the breakers. No registers carry the name of this craft though some sources claimed that it was called *Tillamook.*

Vancouver, British bark, 400 tons, wrecked on the middle sands of the Columbia bar, May 8, 1848, without loss of life. Pilot S. C. Reeves, the first officially appointed bar pilot on the lower Columbia, took charge of the ship when she arrived off the river mouth inbound to Fort Vancouver from London. Captain Mouatt, master of the *Vancouver,* had his men stand by the lead lines, but the pilot assured him that he could make the crossing with his eyes closed. The currents and the freshets were exceptionally strong on that day, and the vessel drifted from her course and hung up on the middle sands. That night, strong winds sent high breakers into the stranded bark and after every conceivable attempt to refloat her had failed, all hands abandoned in the boats and managed to reach the shore without serious mishap. The vessel was owned by the Hudson's Bay Company, and was loaded with agricultural machinery and general stores for the post at Fort Vancouver. Among the cargo was much finery and clothing that was salvaged by the natives. The ladies' gowns and trinkets were appropriated by the Clatsops, who were frequently seen picking berries in the latest London fashions of 1848. Captain Mouatt charged negligence on the part of pilot Reeves, but no further action was taken, and the insurance companies paid for the loss of the vessel.

Vandalia, American bark, washed ashore north of Cape Disappointment, January 9, 1853. Nine lives were lost in the tragedy. (See story, page 102.)

Vazlav Vorovsky, Russian steamship, 4,793 tons, stranded on Peacock Spit, April 3, 1941, without loss of life. (See story page 74.)

W. B. Scranton, American bark, stranded on the middle sands of the Columbia bar, May 5, 1866. The vessel, under Captain Paul Corno, was bound for Portland from San Francisco with 810 tons of cargo valued at $200,000. While sailing into the river, the wind failed and the vessel drifted on the spit at 10 a.m. Captain J. D. Munson, lighthouse keeper at Cape Hancock (Disappointment), went to the rescue with a lifeboat and picked up Captain Paul Corno's wife and a woman passenger, but the crew remained with the ship until nightfall and then abandoned her. She broke up twenty-four hours after she struck the spit, and a few damaged threshing machines were about all of the cargo that was saved. The *Scranton* was valued at $25,000, but was insured for only $9000, and her owner-master had expended $6000 in repairs before departing San Francisco. Corno also owned the bark *Industry,* lost in the same area the previous year.

W. H. Besse, American bark, 1,300 tons, wrecked on Peacock Spit, July 23, 1886, without loss of life. Captain Gibbs, master, stood in for Cape Hancock, until by cross bearings, the bar was three quarters mile distant. Towards evening he tried to stand out to sea, but before the wind filled the canvas, the vessel struck hard on Peacock Spit. Hundreds of persons gathered on the Cape to watch the operations as the rescue crews paced the beach below. The surf mounted, and fear was felt for the eighteen man crew. The bark was loaded with rails, valued at $75,000, for the Northern Pacific Railroad. The vessel itself was valued at $45,000. Her crew finally managed to escape the wreck in the boats, but experienced a rugged ordeal before they reached the beach. The location of the wreck is still marked today with a channel marker, known as Besse Buoy. At the time of the loss, the bark was inbound from New York for Portland. Many observers claimed that Captain Gibbs was attempting to enter the river without the aid of a pilot. Part of the wreck later drifted on the beach a mile north of Ocean Park.

Washington, American steam schooner, 539 tons, stranded on Peacock Spit, November 17, 1911, and was removed in a daring rescue attempt. (See story, page 88.)

Web Foot, American barkentine, 361 tons, abandoned by

her crew in sinking condition off Tillamook Rock Light, November 21, 1904, after being buffeted by a severe gale. The crew reached shore safely, but the vessel plunged to the bottom several hours later. She was built at North Bend, Oregon, in 1869, for A. M. Simpson of San Francisco.

Welsh Prince, British steamship, 5000 tons, collided with the American freighter *Iowan,* off Altoona Head, near Grays Bay, May 28, 1922, with a loss of seven lives. (See story, page 99.)

Whistler, American bark, 820 tons, wrecked on North Beach Peninsula, October 27, 1883. The vessel was bound for Astoria from San Pedro, in ballast. Her skipper was Captain J. F. Soule. Thick weather and strong currents caused the vessel to over run the river entrance and go ashore at 2:30 a.m., on the sands of the Peninsula, south of Ocean Park. In the inquiry over the loss of the vessel, Captain Soule testified that his unfamiliarity with the coastline and the natural forces of the area was responsible for the wreck. The vessel was valued at $18,000, and was built on the Atlantic Coast in 1853.

Whitney Olson, American steam schooner, 1,558 tons, stranded on Clatsop Spit, December 16, 1940, and was saved from destruction by the Coast Guard cutter *Onondaga,* which braved shallow waters and got a line on the lumber freighter. The vessel stranded after dragging her anchors with a jammed rudder. After three hours on the shoals, the cutter towed her off the beach, stern first and took her to Astoria. At the time of the accident, the vessel was bound for Knappton from Los Angeles Harbor.

William and Ann, British bark, 300 tons, wrecked on Clatsop Spit, March 10, 1829, with an estimated loss of forty-six lives. Some accounts claimed the loss of life to have been 26. (See story, page 19.)

William Nottingham, American schooner, 1,204 tons, dismasted and waterlogged in a gale off the Columbia River, October 9, 1911. Her crew were picked up by the schooner *David Evans.* Later the derelict was found by the tug *Wallula* and towed to Astoria as a prize. She underwent extensive repairs and returned to the sealanes. At the time of the accident, the *Nottingham* was outbound for Callao from Astoria. She was built at Ballard, Washington, for the Globe Navigation Company in 1902. Her latter years were spent as a cable barge, and in 1948, she was towed to the mouth of the Nisqually River, on Puget Sound, and sunk as a breakwater.

Windward, American ship, 818 tons, stranded momentarily near Sand Island, December 23, 1871, but was freed after anxious moments. She was inbound for Portland from Seattle when she got caught in a gale off the mouth of the Columbia, along with two other sailing ships. Braving the sou'wester, a tug put out from Astoria and took the *Windward* in tow. The tug towed the ship as far as Sand Island, where she dropped anchor while the tow - boat went out after the other vessels. The wind reached hurricane velocity and the *Windward* drifted toward the island over which a high sea was running. Both anchors were out, but regardless the vessel went on the shoal. The three masts were cut away, which relieved the vessel's burden. She drifted free and was afterwards towed to Portland and fitted with new masts and rigging. She was wrecked for good on Puget Sound four years later.

Woodpecker, British schooner, 300 tons, stranded on Clatsop Spit, May 10, 1861, without loss of life. The vessel was outbound from the Columbia with flour, general freight and 104 head of cattle destined for Victoria, B. C. In transit the schooner missed stays, and the pilot, Captain Alfred Crosby, ordered the anchors dropped immediately to keep the ship from going on the sands. The starboard cable snapped and the *Woodpecker* swung broadside to the breakers, striking in ten feet of water. Over the side went the cattle and the cargo to lighten the ship's burden, but the vessel had punctured her timbers and made water fast. The crew was forced to man the boats and was subsequently picked up by the pilot schooner *California.* Beachcombers reaped a harvest from the sea in the aftermath of the wreck. Only one cow reached shore alive, and she was landed through the efforts of William Chance, an early pioneer of the area. The cow lived for many years but was often accused of having salt water in its milk. The *Woodpecker* was a composite schooner built in England, and valued at $15,000.

Zampa, American schooner, 385 tons, stranded on Point Leadbetter, just south of Willapa Harbor entrance, July 17, 1904, without loss of life. The schooner was buffeted by a gale off the Columbia, and lost her rudder. She commenced drifting at the mercy of the wind and was carried through the breakers. Grounding on the sands, the vessel was 300 feet from the water when the tide ebbed. Captain Kellenberger, his wife and the crew of nine were all saved. For several months the schooner remained on the beach, and after being given up for lost on several occasions, was finally refloated and towed to port for repairs. After a hectic career, the *Zampa* was lost in 1926, near Honolulu. She was built in 1887.

In addition to the foregoing list, several other ocean-going vessels have suffered minor mishaps in and around the Pacific's Graveyard, either through stranding on shoals or from the action of the bar in extreme conditions.

Old U. S. Lifesaving Service records once kept in the stations of the Pacific's Graveyard, are full of small boat strandings. Most of these vessels were between three and five tons, and were unnamed. They for the most part were units of the local fishing fleets. These casualties are too numerous to list, but some of the better known work boats lost in this area are recorded here. All of these craft were under twenty-five tons.

Arrow No. 2, bar tug, 14 tons, exploded and burned off Astoria, January 21, 1949, with the loss of one life.

Beaver, gas screw, 14 tons, stranded on Clatsop Spit, August 3, 1940, without loss of life.

Donna, fish boat, 20 tons, wrecked near Ocean Park, April 14, 1944, with the loss of three lives.

Eine, launch, lost on the Columbia River bar, in September, 1914, without loss of life.

Friendly, fish boat, 17 tons, foundered off the mouth of the Columbia, August 15, 1945.

Jupiter, fish boat, 14 tons, foundered off Willapa Bay, April 14, 1918, with the loss of her crew of four. Her skipper was Captain Charles B. Ammerman.

LaBelle, troller, 15 tons, foundered off Peacock Spit, with the loss of one life, March 25, 1945.

Lenore, troller, 13 tons, stranded near Ocean Park, April 10, 1917, without loss of life.

M. F. Hazen, launch, capsized off the Columbia River bar, in 1905.

Marie, gas boat, foundered off Peacock Spit in the summer of 1913.

Nola, gas screw, stranded on the north spit of Willapa bar, July 29, 1944, without loss of life.

Oregon, launch, lost on the Columbia bar, in the fall of 1914.

Picaroon, fish boat, 9 tons, wrecked on the south jetty of the Columbia River bar, August 17, 1945.

Red Star, gas screw, 21 tons, burned at Warrenton, Oregon, October 14, 1947.

Sea Lion, oil screw, 8 tons, stranded on the Columbia bar, October 5, 1939, without loss of life.

Sea Lion, troller, disappeared with her two man crew off Willapa Bay in calm weather in June, 1948.

Treo, gar screw, 24 tons, foundered off Peacock Spit, December 2, 1940. The crew were saved. The vessel was built in 1914.

29 C 822, troller, wrecked off Clatsop Spit in May, 1944, with the loss of her two crew members.